Contents

Contents

Acknowledgements

We are grateful to the following for permission to reproduce copyright material:

George Allen & Unwin Ltd for extracts from *Equality* by R. H. Tawney; The Gallop Poll for Table 14 and summarised passages from *Voters, Parties and Leaders* by J. Blondel; Cambridge University Press for a short extract from *The Affluent Worker* by Goldthorpe *et al.*; Conservative Political Centre for Table 13 from the article 'Class Distinction in Britain' by M. Abrams as appeared in *The Future of the Welfare State* published by the CPC in 1958, an extract from *The Tory Tradition* (1957) by G. Butler, extracts from *Conservatism Today* (1966) by Peregrine Worsthorne and quotations from *Some Principles of Conservatism* by R. Goldman; Prentice-Hall Inc., for an extract from *The Economics of J. M. Keynes* (1966) by D. Dillard; The Economist Intelligence Unit Limited for small extracts from the report on the National Newspaper Industry prepared by the Economist Intelligence Unit Ltd; Faber & Faber Ltd for extracts from *Liberty in the Modern State* by H. J. Laski; Fabian Society to quote statistics from *Labour and Inequality* ed. by Townsend and Bosanquet; University of Cambridge, Faculty of Economics and Politics for the reference made to *The London & Cambridge Economic Service — Key Statistics*; Gerald Duckworth & Co. Ltd for a brief extract from *The Labour Government's Economic Record: 1964–1970* ed. by Prof. W. Beckerman (Duckworth, London, 1972); William Heinemann Ltd for an extract from *A Woman's World* by Lady Edith Summerskill; Her Majesty's Stationery Office for an extract from *Monthly Digest of Statistics*, for extracts from 'Employment Policy' Cmd. 6527 and for extracts from

Hansard's *Parliamentary Debates*, Vol. 803/4; David Higham Associates Ltd for short extracts from Speeches quoted in *The New Britain* by Harold Wilson; Hutchinson Publishing Group Ltd for a brief extract from *The Body Politic* by Ian Gilmour; Independent Labour Party for an extract from *Socialism for Today* by H. N. Brailsford; The Labour Party for a summarised quotation from the pamphlet *The Social Services* 1968 by the Labour Party; Penguin Books Ltd for extracts from *May Day Manifesto* (1968) ed. by Raymond Williams © by May Day Manifesto Committee 1968, and, for short extracts from *Political Theory and Practice* by Bernard Crick (Allen Lane The Penguin Press, 1972) Reprinted by Permission of Penguin Books Ltd; the author and MacGibbon & Kee for extracts from *Working Class Tories* (1967) by Eric Allen Nordlinger; Authors' Agents for short extracts from *Influencing Voters* by Richard Rose. Reprinted by permission of A. D. Peters and Company; Tom Stacey Ltd for extracts from *For Conservatives Only* by Lord Coleraine. Copyright © 1970 Tom Stacey Ltd; St. Martin's Press Inc. and Macmillan, London and Basingstoke for Table 4.7 and extracts from *Political Change in Britain* by D. Butler and D. Stokes and Times Newspapers Ltd for a summary of the BBC report of Standards in BBC and a summary of the Budget Speeches by Roy Jenkins in *The Times*, 15.4.70.

We are grateful to the following for permission to reproduce photographs: Popperfoto for page 185 and the frontispiece; Syndication International for page 145; *Sunday Mirror* for page 185; *Radio Times* Hulton Picture Library for page 123; Keystone for page 49; Harlow Urban District Council public relations office for page 65; The Labour Party for page 173.

Preface

To the teacher or lecturer using this book

This book is intended for the more intelligent trainees, apprentices and technicians in the Engineering and Technical Departments, the full time general education and commercial students and the now numerous nursing and social-work students to be found in Colleges of Further Education. Approaching 17–18 years of age, many of them are looking for information that will help them to make up their minds as voters in the not-so-distant future. Others, already interested in public affairs and politics are looking for 'straight' information on the Parties and their policies and an opportunity to discuss them free from party propaganda.

The book should prove useful, also, in secondary schools and sixth form colleges where extended attendance calls for studies even more closely related to events in the adult world than have hitherto been provided. It could be tackled by senior students as a non-examination study, with a limited amount of teacher guidance, and lead to useful extra-curricular activity.

The book makes a very practical approach, attempting to answer questions that arise naturally in the minds of healthily sceptical youth: Why do we have Government, they ask? What does the Government do? Isn't Parliament just a talking shop? Why do we have Political Parties? Is there any difference between them? Isn't it all beyond me — out of the reach of ordinary people? The author's aim is not only to give information but to help the reader understand what is going on and encourage him to discuss the issues that puzzle so many of us today.

The course outlined in the book would fit well into a scheme of studies dealing with the social, economic and political aspects of our lives. Part 1 of the book (on government) could make up the third term's work for first year students and Part 2 (on politics) take a similar position in the second year. This would avoid giving students too heavy a dose of government and politics at one time and enable the teacher to link the study to related social and economic questions.

The subjects for discussion at the end of each chapter have been tried out over a number of years and are offered with some confidence. Of course, as every experienced teacher knows (sadly), not every topic comes to life with every group. But from the many topics offered, a teacher should have little difficulty in selecting some to suit his group and should not find it beyond his wit to illustrate them from current happenings. Nor, with a good knowledge of his locality and its politics will he be at a loss to supplement the suggestions 'for action'.

The book does not pretend to cover examination syllabuses in government and British Constitution. Its purpose, as noted, is other. Nevertheless, GCE and other students may well find it a useful – and it is to be hoped, stimulating – introduction to their subject.

The author wishes to thank his former colleagues at the North London College for Further Education, the Southwark College for Further Education and the London College of Printing for numerous helpful suggestions and sage advice given in innumerable chats and discussions in the staff room. His debt to the students of these institutions is even greater. Their initial indifference and earthy scepticism have been a challenge: their enthusiasm, when and if aroused, an encouragement and reward.

The author also wishes to thank Mr Tom Brennan, of the Bingley College of Education, for encouragement and advice, given with such unfailing and entertaining good humour, over many years: and to Val Bynner, for reading the script and giving much helpful advice. The Rt. Hon. J. Enoch Powell, MBE, MP, kindly consented to the quotations made in Chapter 16 from some of his speeches and was good enough, in a busy life, to suggest some useful improvements in the script relating to them.

Introduction

To the reader

This book is written principally for young people coming up to voting age who wish to inform themselves about the political system in which they are about to take part.

It notes that there are people who, for one reason or another, reject all government action, and their views are considered. It is rather for those who take the common-sense view that *some* government is necessary and ask how much is necessary at any time and what it is that determines what is a reasonable amount.

It looks at the system we have in this country, 'democracy', or government by the people. It notes that in a large nation like ours all the citizens cannot personally take part in the details of law-making. We therefore elect people to act for us and have evolved, over the years, a system of 'representative' democracy. The book then asks what conditions must exist before a nation can properly call itself a democracy. It outlines them in terms of certain 'freedoms' — freedom of speech, freedom of the press, freedom to join with others in organising political parties and other associations, freedom from arrest without cause. It looks back over the last 150 years to see how the right to vote was won and to note that, as the franchise widened, so did the field of government activity.

Next, the book looks at a general election which normally takes place at least once in five years and notes how the decision of the electors results in the formation of a government. We see, then, how the procedures of Parliament provide checks against the abuse of power by the government and how the ordinary citizen can exert influence on his Member of Parliament. We note here that Parliament, aware of the danger of excessive government power, has established watchdogs, such as the Ombudsman, and tribunals, to whom and to which the ordinary citizen may appeal if he thinks that someone, acting in the name of the government, has infringed his rights. We also take a brief look at the Law as a protector of individual liberty.

Part 1 ends with a glance at the methods of government employed in some other countries, taking warning or encouragement when comparing our system with theirs.

In Part 2 we look at the political parties, asking if they are necessary. Yes, we answer, because without them our democratic system would not work.

Given, then, that parties are necessary, what do the principal political parties in this country stand for? Are there any real differences between them today? We examine their basic attitudes and note that there are differences. Why, then, we ask, do they act so similarly in tackling so many of today's problems? We note here the revolution between today's methods and those used before the war — especially in the attempts of all governments to avoid mass unemployment and to secure a steadily rising standard of life for all of us.

The section ends with a look at the influences that push us this way and that in our choice of a party. It asks what we can do to make that choice more reasonable — by being better informed on party policies, on the problems that all governments have to face and the means available for their solution.

Throughout the book there is emphasis on discussion. Each chapter ends with questions for readers to argue about. But though argument is an essential part of democracy, it is not an end in itself. Unless it leads to action — in the innumerable ways mentioned throughout the book — it is a mere indulgence. The book ends, then, with a plea for greater participation.

Democracy, said Abraham Lincoln, is government of the people, by the people, for the people. Unless we, the people, do take part, there is no real democracy. Sham democracy too easily gives way to dictatorship. Taking part, then, is not only a duty but a necessity: and, as this book seeks to show, not a dull but an interesting and even exciting one.

The Houses of Parliament

Part 1

You and your government

Chapter 1

Government: a necessity

1.1 Government is necessary

Many people today talk as though government is not necessary. Government is authoritarian, they say. It is oppressive. Politicians are out for power: they make us do what *they* want, not what *we* want to do. We are restricted at every turn. We can't put up a garage without someone's consent. We can't drive above 70 mph on the motorway or get a drink after 11 pm. We can't even spend our money as we like. The government takes it from us and spends it as *it* thinks. There is too much government nowadays. We'd be better off without any government — or at least with very much less.

Against this are the people who say that civilised life and organised society depend on the existence of governments: that without government it would be every man for himself with the strong and ruthless getting rich and the rest of us trodden under foot. Government, say these people, safeguards our liberties.

Where does the truth lie? Somewhere in between! The fact is we grumble at what the government does but demand its help when we are in trouble. If the firm where we work closes down, we ask what the government is doing about all this unemployment. If we haven't a house we ask why the government doesn't order the local council to build more. A woman is dying because she cannot afford a kidney machine: why doesn't the Health Service provide it? Farmers want more money, teachers more pay. There's a flood in Devon, oil slick on the beach at Brighton, a coal tip on the move in Wales. What is the government going to do about it?

Why this contradiction in our attitudes? Mainly because we have a one-sided view of what government does. We notice it only when it affects us unfavourably and take for granted all that it contributes to our well-being.

All societies must have rules. Only the solitary man — Adam before the arrival of Eve, the lone castaway on the tropical island — can do exactly as he likes. When Eve arrived Adam had to take into consideration her needs, her likes and dislikes. Of course her arrival brought some advantages. Their price was the consideration he had to give to her. All society brings advantages in the form of opportunities to live a richer life than we can live on our own. The price we pay is the limit to our freedom to do exactly as we like. We have to weigh the advantages against the disadvantages.

1.2 The government's job

What do we expect a modern government to do? In fact, we expect a great deal. We expect security in the street and at football matches. We expect security for our house and property. People who steal cars and wantonly damage motor-bicycles should be dealt with severely, we say. We demand that criminals should be restrained. There must be courts to deal with law-breakers, and the 'forces of law and order' — the police — to stand behind the law. Then there is the 'Civil Law', that provides opportunities for us to settle our differences without resort to violence. Here we are concerned less with dishonesty than with genuine differences between one person and another. We may have trouble over debts due to us, over hire-purchase arrangements, over the quality of goods bought and sold. A married couple may want a divorce. We may disagree with the boss over the terms of our contract of employment. We take these disputes to the 'civil' courts, rights and wrongs are thrashed out and a settlement arrived at.

There are many rules to ensure that we behave decently towards our neighbour — and that he behaves decently towards us. Thus, I may not slander him — nor he, me. I must not make his life miserable by carrying on an offensive trade, or allow my house to be infested by rats or lice. I mustn't spread infectious diseases. I mustn't disturb my neighbour by yelling my head off on the way home from the pub on Saturday night. I musn't drive on the right-hand side of the road when everyone else agrees to drive on the left. I may not use certain language in public nor offend my neighbour's religious susceptibilities. I mustn't discriminate against anyone on grounds of race. Most of us can see that we gain more than we lose by these 'rules' which limit our freedom of action. Many of them are based on custom and come down to us

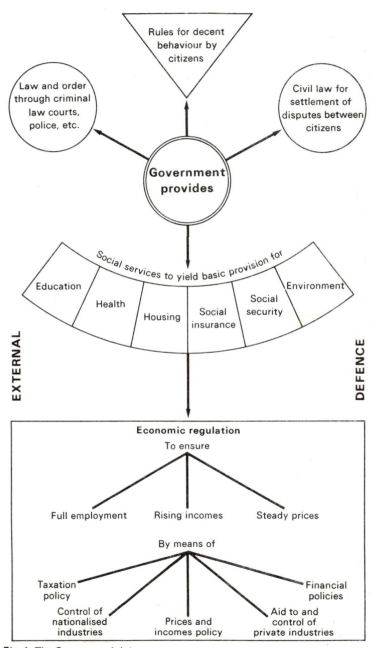

Fig. 1 The Government's job

through the 'common law', but what is thought to be proper behaviour changes from time to time, and governments act to bring the rules up to date. For example, the Divorce Laws were changed in 1969 and homosexual acts between consenting male adults ceased to be an offence in 1967. Usually Parliament lags behind public opinion in making these changes: sometimes, as in the abolition of the death penalty in 1969, it acts in advance of it.

Since the beginning of this century we have expected governments to provide us more and more with the basic requirements of a decent life: education, a health service, housing; a minimum cash income if we are sick, unemployed, widowed, or too old to keep at work. Since the Second World War governments have gone a step further. They not only see that an unemployed man is kept out of want: they are expected to ensure that unemployment itself is kept at a minimum. Between the wars it averaged 12—20 per cent of the working population. Since the war it has been kept to between 1½ and 3½ per cent. To achieve this, governments have had to interfere much more in economic (that is business) matters than they did before the war. All parties are pledged to maintain a 'high and stable level of employment'. They are very much concerned about 'the balance of payments', that is, the relation between imports and exports, and are blamed if our standard of living does not rise as steadily or as fast as we think it should. More recently attention has been focused on the '*cost* of living'. We have been used to prices rising steadily since the end of the war, but when they shoot up by 10 per cent in a year (as they did in 1970) we become alarmed and angry and blame the government.

Beyond these home affairs is the question of external defence. We expect our government to keep the armed forces in such a state that we and our allies are secure against attack. This is an expensive business in a world dominated by nuclear weapons. We may argue about the allies we should have and the weapons necessary: few people argue that we should have none.

1.3 How much government ?

Granted that government is necessary, how much do we need at any time? Looking back into history we can see that there were times when governments limited their activities to very narrow fields: at other times they acted much more extensively. Why was this? Was it because 'they' — the people who governed — liked power and couldn't resist interfering in our affairs?

Not altogether. Undoubtedly there is always a danger that people in power will come to like exercising it and want more. We have to make sure that there are checks on the unwarranted use of power, as Chapter 7 shows. No. There appear to be two main factors which determine the extent of government involvement at any time: the first is the way we organise our economic life, that is, the way we produce the food and other commodities on which we live. The second is our ideas of right and wrong, of what is tolerable or intolerable; the extent to which we think that society itself should concern itself in these affairs.

(a) Economic change and government regulation

Take economic affairs. Obviously a country with a simple economic organisation will require few and simple rules. An African tribe that lives by grazing cattle, moving on as pastures become exhausted, will need rules about the size of herds, rights of water and wood, about who is entitled to the limited grazing. (Our forefathers lived like this in Britain 10,000 years ago.) With more settled cultivation, the question of land tenure arose. On what terms could a man claim exclusive use of a piece of land? In feudal times in Britain a man 'paid' for his land by service to the Lord of the Manor. In medieval towns Guilds — organisations of craftsmen — regulated clothmaking, brewing, baking, the making of soap and pottery and so on. The Guilds determined the number of apprentices a master could have, supervised apprentice training, determined the quality of the product and fixed prices. Rules were thus made locally, in village or town.

But as trade and industry expanded and local regulations by the Guilds broke down (for example, as the more go-ahead masters moved out of their jurisdiction and into new areas) the Tudor and early Stuart monarchs passed laws to continue the traditional regulation of industry so that regulation, like industry and trade itself, was now nation wide.

The Statute of Apprentices (1563) insisted on the proper training of apprentices. It empowered Justices of the Peace to fix maximum wages in each locality 'to yield unto the hired person both in time of scarcity and the time of plenty a convenient proportion of wages'— that is, a reasonable living wage. Employers were pressed to keep their men at work in times of slack trade. The State regulated technical processes, the quality of raw materials, the style of the finished product. Overseas trade was encouraged. Exports were helped by 'bounties' or bonuses; imports, including corn, were taxed to keep them to a minimum. Britain became nearly self-supporting.

People who complain today about government interference in industry forget — or do not know — that in one of our greatest periods of history, the Elizabethan, regulation of industry and trade was widespread and taken for granted.

(b) The end of regulation and the growth of free enterprise

A change came after the Civil War (1642–52). Employers were no longer required to keep their workmen in times of bad trade. Apprenticeship lost its legal status and employers brought in unskilled and poorly paid labourers to take the place of skilled men. Regulations that had held back development in industry and trade were abolished. Competition at home and free trade abroad were advocated as the recipe for rapid expansion. Adam Smith, a Scotsman, brought these ideas together in a book *The Wealth of Nations* (1775) which did much to make them acceptable. The competitive struggle of one manufacturer with another was no longer to be seen as the pursuit of greedy self-interest: it was competition in service. And as one man strove to maximise his own wealth, he was 'led by an invisible hand to promote an end that was no part of his intention', [1] * that is, the maximisation of the wealth of the whole of society. For this beneficent (and as Adam Smith would say) 'natural' state to exist there must be competition and above all, no government interference with individual enterprise. The policy of *laissez-faire* ('let be', or 'leave alone') was adopted as the best policy for the country.

It worked. Released from government control, machine and factory production expanded as never before. Britain's coal and iron resources were exploited. Steam power replaced muscle-power. New industries grew up, new towns developed, crowded with labourers no longer required on the land or in handcraft industries. 'During its reign of scarce one-hundred years,' wrote Karl Marx, a critic of this process, in 1848, the new manufacturing class 'has created more massive and more colossal productive forces than have all preceding generations together'. [2] Nature's forces were being rapidly subjected by man, chemistry applied to industry and agriculture, steam navigation and railways expanded, new continents cleared for cultivation, 'whole populations conjured out of the ground' — what earlier century had dreamed that such forces existed?

True, the new towns were often insanitary and without supplies of water. True, adults and children were being savagely used in factories and coal-mines. Protests against these conditions were made but the belief in *laissez-faire* — leave alone — prevailed over calls for remedial action. The dominant belief was that Parliament must not interfere.

(c) The return of regulation

As the nineteenth century proceeded the public conscience was stirred over the treatment of children in industry and Parliament was eventually pursuaded to regulate the conditions under which they worked.

* Figures in square brackets indicate list of references at the end of book (p. 194).

Children were banned from the coal-mines. Women's conditions of work were regulated and as a consequence, men's also. Predictions that disaster would flow from this interference by Parliament in the 'natural order' were not fulfilled. In fact, production expanded and trade flourished. The sanitary condition of towns was tackled. Trade unions were legalised. In the early twentieth century insurance against old age, sickness and unemployment were provided by the State. Taxation was increased to pay for these 'social services'.

In the inter-war years (1918—39) Britain went through a series of economic crises. Older industries like coal-mining, shipbuilding and textiles were declining. Other countries penetrated our export markets. There were up to 3 million unemployed. From all sides there were demands that the government should intervene more in economic affairs. Conservatives wanted 'protection' for industry; that is, taxes on the import of manufactured goods so that we could manufacture them for ourselves. Socialists called for the nationalisation of the basic industries so that they could be reorganised and run in the nation's interest, not that of the owners. Economists like J. M. (later Lord) Keynes urged that the government should increase its spending on roads, houses, schools, etc., so that the unemployed be brought back into work.

These proposals were resisted at the time but the Second World War (1939—45) jolted us out of our old ways of thinking. Since 1945 all governments have intervened extensively in economic affairs. The basic industries have been nationalised. Imports are regulated. Governments act to ensure a 'high and stable level of employment'.

(d) The influence of ideas

We have seen that changing economic circumstances produce problems which governments are expected to deal with. *How* they deal with them depends on the ideas dominant at the time. What shapes this 'climate of opinion'? We have noted the influence of thinkers like Adam Smith and Lord Keynes who produced theories which altered the whole scope of government action. There have also been people whose concern was a single problem or injustice. In the early nineteenth century Lord Shaftesbury agitated for better working conditions in industry. Edwin Chadwick forced through the operation of public health acts that cleaned up our towns. Church people of all denominations provided education for the masses. Trade unionists fought for better wages and an improved status for the workers. Investigators like Seebohm Rowntree, Charles Booth, Sidney and Beatrice Webb exposed poverty in our great cities and led the demand for reform. Eleanor Rathbone campaigned for twenty years for family allowances. Harold Macmillan (Conservative) and Ellen Wilkinson (Labour) fought in Parliament for a new attitude towards unemployment. There were countless others who pioneered changes in education, the provision of nursery schools, school meals and medicals, aid to old people, baby clinics: one could fill a page. These people, working alone or through voluntary organisations and political parties, changed people's thinking and brought pressure to bear on the government of the day so that action was taken.

This process continues. Indeed, it is probable that there were never so many people with so many concerns pressing action on the government as there are today. Their work is noted frequently in the course of this book. There are, also, people who want less government. Between them, they influence the way we think, and what we do to persuade the government to act as we want it to.

Many people think that they can have no personal influence on this process; that what they say doesn't count. In fact, it does count, as this book shows.

In the next chapter we consider *our* form of government: democracy. In later chapters we examine its working and particularly the part that can be played by the ordinary well-informed citizen. Meanwhile we consider some important questions raised by this chapter.

Questions *for discussion and action*

1. While we would all agree that the regulation to drive on the left side of the road interferes very little with individual 'freedom' and the gain is overwhelming, consider the following 'restrictions':
    (a) The speed limit;
    (b) The breathaliser rules;
    (c) Penalties for driving when the breathaliser reveals a certain percentage of alcohol in the blood;
    (d) Parking regulations.
    Do you think they are justified?
2. Would you make any regulations (such as crossing the road only at certain points) compulsory for pedestrians? Give examples.
3. The law compels parents to send children to school (unless they can provide an adequate education at home). Is this compulsion an infringement of individual liberty? Why should we not have the right to remain ignorant?
4. A great deal of social control is exercised by 'Society' direct and not through actual laws. There are 'unwritten' laws as well as written. These work through 'social pressures', exerted by one's family, friends, the neighbours. Discuss actual examples.
5. The taking of certain drugs is prohibited by law: Why? Alcohol is also a drug. Should drinking alcohol be prohibited? (It was in the United States for a short period.) Smoking is injurious. Should it be prohibited? The advertising of cigarettes is banned on TV and

otherwise restricted. Would you prohibit all tobacco advertisements?

6. The advertisement of patent medicines is restricted. Is this an intolerable restriction on liberty?

7. Reviewing your answers to the above questions can you sum up your attitudes by completing the following sentence:

    It is proper for the state to legislate to limit the individual's absolute right to do as he wishes when:

    (a) Social pressures are insufficient;

    (b) Harm may otherwise come to a person too young to be able to judge his own long-term interests;

    (c)

    (d)

    etc.

8. How far do you go with the statement that 'Freedom involves the right of the individual to make mistakes and injure himself if he wishes to. He may even take his own life'.

9. Name organisations working today to change people's opinions and through that, government action on:

    (a) Houses for homeless people;

    (b) Aid for underdeveloped countries;

    (c) Poor children in this country;

    (d) Unmarried mothers;

    (e) Spastics;

    (f) The mentally ill.

    Can you think of people who need help but for whom no one seems to care?

    Send for information on the activities of any organisation in whose work you are interested. Report to your group on it.

Chapter 2

Our system of democracy

We claim that we are a Democracy. What do we mean by that? The word comes from the Greek, meaning rule by the people. In ancient Greek City States there was direct democracy. The people (i.e. the freemen, though not the slaves) gathered in one place, such as the Pnyx at Athens, a semi-circular terrace cut from the hillside about 500 yards east of the Acropolis, to discuss questions of government. All took part. In some cities, office was taken in turn or by ballot. This direct democracy was possible because there were few citizens and all could meet in one place. Now that we live in such great numbers there are too many of us to go to Parliament. We now choose people to represent us in Parliament, to make laws on our behalf, to carry on the business of government. This system is called *in*direct, or representative democracy.

At once, difficulties arise. Who shall take part in the choosing or election of these representatives? How shall we ensure that, once elected, they act as we wish? How can we replace a representative who no longer has our confidence? How can we ensure that they have sufficient power to be effective in running our affairs yet not so much that they can impose their will upon us in ways we do not wish? How can we ensure that the Civil Service, who assemble the complicated technical information on which decisions are made, do not become a power in themselves? How can we ensure that 'the people' in whom power ultimately lies, have the wisdom to use it well and not ill?

It is to secure 'Government by the People' in this sense and to meet these difficulties that our present system of government, less than perfect though it is, has been built up.

Strangely enough, although we pride ourselves on being a democracy, our system of government contains some apparently non-democratic elements: for example, where do the Queen and the House of Lords fit in, since the former entirely and the latter partially depend on hereditary right? These anomalies are dealt with later when the operation of the system of law-making is described: it is sufficient here to say that the powers of the Queen and the Lords have been reduced and made subject to the overriding power of the Commons. They contribute in numerous ways to the smooth running of government.

What, then, are the basic essentials of any genuinely democratic government?

2.1 Votes for all

First, we believe that all the people and not only the top people should have a say. Hence we have established an electoral system under which each adult has one vote — and only one. (The evolution of this system is described in Chapter 3.) A further requirement is that there should be means by which citizens can keep a check on their representatives and get rid of them if they wish. (This is discussed in Chapter 8.)

2.2 The assertion of freedoms

Another requirement of democracy is that we should have certain 'freedoms' — freedom of speech so that we can discuss the way our government behaves, exchange ideas with other people, argue out our differences; have free access to information through a free press, radio and television; freedom to join trade unions, professional groups, business associations and other groups that further our particular interests; freedom to join other people and groups in political parties to work out the policies we think best for the nation, freedom to publicise them and put up candidates to support them, with a view to securing power in Parliament to carry them out. We need freedom from arrest without cause and equality before the law. A country without these freedoms is, we say, not a democracy.

2.3 Freedom of speech

To what extent have we a free press and freedom of speech? We must note first that there are no absolute freedoms. Only Adam (as we noted earlier) was completely free and that only for a short time. We can say what we like *but*:

> We must not slander another; that is, tell untruths about him and so rob him of his character.

> We must not utter certain obscenities or blasphemies. Here the limits are changing. Certain four-letter words may now be printed, heard on television and presumably spoken in public.

> We may not say anything to invoke racial hatred or prejudice. (This is a new prohibition.)

In political matters, though, we have a wide tolerance. We may say what we like about the government, we may question its policies and advocate alternative ones; we may tell it to go. May we urge violence to overthrow it? Yes, even this, if it is done discreetly — in writing. What we may not do is actually to commission, or commit violence. The police can act immediately there is a 'breach of the peace' or stop action 'likely to lead to a breach of the peace'. It may seem illogical to permit an article in a select journal advocating violence but not a direct command to violence at the street corner. It is a risk taken so as to preserve, as far as possible, freedom of the written word. Some people opposed the bill prohibiting incitement to racial hatred on the grounds that it limited freedom of speech, but the majority thought that the loss of this freedom was outweighed by the benefit, the lessening of racial tension that it hoped would result.

2.4 Freedom of the press

Have we a free press? We have in the sense that our newspapers are not the mere mouthpieces of governments or their associated parties as in totalitarian States where all organs of information or propaganda are in the hands of one party and government. Our newspapers are free to publish what they wish and express what views they wish, within the laws of libel, decency and racial hatred: and the requirements of national security.

This is not to say that all points of view are in fact publicised; but they could be. Theoretically anyone is free to start a new newspaper if he thinks that a point of view needs publicity: free, that is, if he has the necessary capital — say a million pounds. In practice it is very difficult to start a new national newspaper, as a number of people have discovered. National newspapers are becoming fewer, local newspapers coming under the control of groups like Lord Thomson's. Does this mean that they are less free? Lord Thomson declares that he does not interfere with his editors — and generally they agree.

Why are there fewer national newspapers? Even some with circulations of over a million a day are thought to be financially insecure. All papers depend on revenue from advertising. The larger the circulation, the more advertisers they attract. Hence the large grow larger and the smaller disappear. Circulation is vital and this may influence what is put in the papers. There must be a lot of entertainment, a good bit of excitement and not too heavy a load of serious information and discussion. Newspapers catering for minority views will be at a disadvantage. It is more difficult for a Labour or Liberal paper to keep going than a Conservative one. Lord Thomson's aim, he says, is profit. Is this compatible with the provision of a press that will continually inform the electorate and lead a serious discussion of important issues? Or does it lead to the trivialisation of politics? Have we a press permanently biased against the 'Left'? Can a democracy be satisfied with newspapers owned almost exclusively by millionaires?

It is easier to ask the questions than answer them. No one in this country suggests the nationalisation of the press though some would like to see an independent national paper run rather like the BBC — State financed but independent of the government. Others suggest an extension of the system under which the *Guardian* and the *Observer* are managed: no owner or shareholder has control but the papers are managed by Trustees (public or representative figures without a financial interest in the paper) who appoint the editor, then leave him editorial freedom. Yet others suggest that existing papers should be bought out and run by certain established interests in society; for example, the political parties, the trade unions (through the TUC), organised industry (through the Confederation of British Industry), the farmers, the retailers, consumers, educationists, artists. This, it is claimed, would enable all substantial points of view to be expressed and give better support for our democratic society than our present plutocratically owned press. The Economist Intelligence Unit, surveying the newspaper industry in 1966 [1] noted 'its dominance by a small number of highly individualistic proprietors with their own personal interests and philosophy of management'. Thus, Lord Thomson's organisation owns *The Times*, *The Sunday Times* and *The Scotsman*. The *Daily Mail* and the *Evening News* are owned by Associated Newspapers Ltd of which 'all important decisions are referred to the proprietor who continues to exercise great influence throughout the organisation and largely dictates the policy to be followed.' Viscount Camrose exerts considerable authority in the affairs of the *Daily Telegraph*. The *Daily Express* and *Evening Standard* are owned by Beaverbrook Newspapers Ltd, which 'have traditionally been used as vehicles for the propagation of the late Lord Beaverbrook's personal philosophy and political ideals'. Since Lord Beaverbrook's death the shares are held by a Trust whose duties are to sustain through the publications of that company the policy of Empire for Trade that it has advocated for many years. Its control is 'firmly in the hand of one man of very considerable ability' [2]. The *Daily Mirror* and *Sunday Mirror* are owned by a large organisation known as the International Publishing Corporation. The *Sun* (formerly the *Daily Herald*, and at one time partly owned by the Trades Union Congress) is owned by Mr Rupert Murdoch, owner of a number of popular Australian newspapers. The *Morning Star* (formerly the *Daily Worker*) is owned by a cooperative society to which many of its readers subscribe and supports the policy of the British Communist Party.

It is sometimes argued that the national newspapers have little influence on politics: that, for instance, the Labour Party rose to power with the mass of the press against it. True, it rose to second place in the inter-war years but in 1945, when it achieved its first real power, it had the support of the powerful *Mirror* as well as its own paper the *Herald*. It is said, further, that the Labour Government's unpopularity in the late 1960s was due, not only to the severe measures it had taken but to a universally hostile press. This is countered by the view that, like advertisements, newspapers cannot sell an unpopular product but merely crystallise already held opinions. Against all these views it is argued that 'we get the press we deserve', that a shallow or sensational press reflects a shallow and irresponsible public. There is some truth in this but only some. The press is not a mere money-making concern. It has a responsibility and acknowledges it. It performs a valuable public service in spreading news and opinions and in exposing scandal.

2.5 Freedom in broadcasting

Both the British Broadcasting Corporation and the independent television companies are expected to provide balanced programmes of a high quality over a wide range of subjects.

Under its charter the BBC is forbidden to broadcast any commercial advertisement and it must broadcast an impartial day by day account of the proceedings of Parliament, which it does in 'Today in Parliament' on Radio 4. It must find room, also, for important statements by government Ministers and provide facilities for broadcasts by political parties. It may not express its own opinion on public matters, and must ensure that its political programmes are balanced and impartial.

The independent television companies, which operate under the Television Act 1964, are required to ensure that 'nothing is included in the programmes which offends against good taste or decency or is likely to encourage or incite or lead to disorder or to be offensive to public feeling', and this is also accepted by the BBC as a standard. An Independent Television Authority has been set up to supervise the contracting companies. A separate company, Independent Television News (ITN), which is a subsidiary of the programme companies, supplies the news.

While both the BBC and independent television have a high reputation for reliability in their news programmes, criticism arises from time to time about discussion programmes and documentaries. Accusations of deliberate bias in these programmes are rarely sustained. But some documentaries are so carefully balanced that they leave a colourless, neutered impression of the issues discussed: viewers are left thinking that its 'six for one and half a dozen for the other' — and the subject is dismissed. Other documentaries arouse strong feelings in the viewers. The question is: do they stimulate further thought and action? Some do, undoubtedly, and this is a gain.

On discussion programmes, too, heat is sometimes generated at the expense of light. A number of excellent chairmen exist who draw out the contestants and maintain reasonable standards of behaviour. Some interviewers, however, try to force views on to the interviewees and ask needling questions; some are concerned only to trap their victims into unguarded statements that will be regretted; and some are almost insulting. Although there are inevitable clashes from time to time between the broadcasting authorities and politicians, there is little sustained complaint.

The broadcasting authorities are in a difficult position when the country is seriously divided on a political issue such as the invasion of Suez in 1956. They are criticised, also, for the amount of time given to religious broadcasting in view of the declining interest of the public in church going. Then there is the presentation of Royalty: some critics hold that the broadcasting authorities are too deferential and should permit criticism. The authorities point out that differences exist among the public on all these issues. Broadcasting has not created them. It merely reflects them.

Granted that there must be some limitations on the programmes shown (as there are limitations on what newspapers may print or what cinemas and theatres may show) can it be argued that the broadcasting authorities are in a special position because their programmes come into people's homes and special care is therefore necessary? Programmes are frequently viewed by the family as a group comprising two and sometimes three generations and if the programmes upset the susceptibilities of *some* of that audience, it may create strains in the family. In a report on 'Taste and Standards in BBC Programmes' [3] issued in February 1973 the BBC accepted the view that 'because of the way in which broadcasting reaches its audience, there are constraints to be observed in the choice of material and its treatment which do not necessarily apply to other means of communication'. There had been complaints about bad language, nudity, sex and violence in programmes. The BBC said that it had a duty to encourage creativity among producers and authors of talent and these frequently took an unorthodox attitude towards sexuality. Heavy control would stifle creativity: absence of control would lead to the giving of a great deal of offence. By avoiding the 'gratuitous' use of nudity and bad language and permitting its use only where it was essential for the furtherance of a dramatic purpose; by putting its exhibition at particular times (when, for example, children might be expected to be in bed) and after a warning about the nature of the programme had been given, it was hoped to avoid giving offence while keeping the programmes open to new ideas.

It is right that the broadcasting authorities should be open to criticism. We can be happy that the BBC and independent television are not the mere mouthpiece of the government as in some countries. Attempted 'pressures' upon them, whether by politicians, or those who seek to preserve moral standards, or at the other extreme, those who oppose the imposition of any censorship, soon come to public notice and the issues are fought out in public.

2.6 Freedom from ignorance and apathy

It is not enough to have freedom of speech, free broadcasting, the right to join a political party, unless we make use of them.

These freedoms had to be fought for: they will continue only to the extent that they are exercised. Professor Crick, well known for his writings on both practical politics and political theory, says [4]:

Freedom depends on people continuing to act freely in public affairs and in being willing to run risks by speaking bluntly in public.

He says further:

Politics is the public action of free men: free men are those who do, not merely can, live both publicly and privately. Men who have lost the capacity for public action, who fear it or despise it, are not free, they are simply isolated and ineffectual.

For effective action, then, we need first, knowledge, then the will to act. These two hang together. The apathetic citizen usually just does not know how to act effectively. The informed citizen does know and frequently wants to.

What can the interested citizen do?

First he can read a newspaper that takes politics seriously and does not personalise, trivialise and sensationalise the news. He should visit the Local and College libraries and dip into the weekly reviews. He should browse along the bookshelves especially section 354/42 on British Government and 942/085, where he will see the biographies of a number of British statesmen he has heard about. He should start building his own personal library by buying paperbacks — say one a week. (Hints on reading are given on p. 189, but personal choice is everything.)

Next he should consider joining one of the political pressure and action groups, such as Shelter or Release or Oxfam already mentioned. There are local branches in most areas.

If he attends a secondary school or college of further education he should ask himself if the current affairs, civics or government studies (if provided at all) are what he wants. Are these studies treated realistically or do the staff 'play safe' and confine the studies to details of 'The British Constitution' rather than the 'dangerous' stuff of politics? He can ask pertinent questions about this.

He may join a political party (though he may not want to at this stage). If he does, he may well find their efforts at political education are feeble or non-existent. The parties issue policy statements and urge discussion on them, but the response is uneven. A request from a new member — especially a young member — for regular talks and discussions on basic issues would be welcomed in most parties.

More serious studies can be undertaken in the foundation courses in the 'Humanities' (Politics, Economics, Sociology) offered by the Open University, Bletchley, Bucks, through a combination of correspondence, broadcast and classroom study.

Reading this book is a start. Subsequent chapters give some information on the system of government and politics practised in this country, party differences are analysed and suggestions made about follow-up action. But first, some of the issues raised in this chapter need discussion.

Questions *for discussion and action*
1. Consider the limits of free speech for the individual person: should we be allowed greater freedom of expression? (Be specific.)
2. Do you think that existing newspapers give an opportunity for the adequate expression of all points of view?
   Consider, especially the case of the following minorities:
   (a) Student protest movements.
   (b) Anarchists.
   (c) Users of cannabis ('pot').
   (d) Drop-outs.
   (e) Homeless families.
   Have any of these groups had more than their share of any other medium of information, such as television or radio?

3. Have you detected bias in any newspaper you read? Give examples. Discuss means for the widening of ownership and control of the press mentioned on p. 15.

4. Analyse the content of one popular paper. (Home news; overseas news; sport; features; gossip; scandal; advertisements.)
   Do you consider the popular newspapers to be trivial?

5. Do you consider the BBC and other television and radio programmes to be biased for or against any particular political party? Illustrate your point of view by specific examples.
   Discuss programmes like 'Panorama' and 'Today', documentaries and feature programmes seen by the group, from the point of view of their usefulness, lack of bias, interest and stimulation to further reading or action.

6. Some people think that the broadcasting authorities should uphold traditional religious views and traditional values in sexual and other behaviour. Others believe that broadcasting should reflect differences on these matters as they exist in society.
   Since challenging views make more exciting broadcasting than the currently accepted views, is there a danger that traditional morality will be undermined and nothing positive put in its place?

7. Consider the arguments for and against the censorship of plays, films, books. Do television programmes come into a different category in that they bring performances into the home?

8. Mr Colin Jordan, the British Fascist, complains that he is prevented from holding meetings because local councils refuse to lend him their premises. Is this a denial of free speech? Is it consistent with our claim to be a democracy?

9. Some students have tried to prevent Mr Enoch Powell from speaking in universities as a protest against his views on immigrants. Is this a denial of free speech? If you disapprove of it as a method of protest, what would you substitute?

10. The following saying is attributed to Voltaire:
    I disapprove of what you say, but I will defend to the death your right to say it.
    Do you feel the same passion for freedom of speech? (Some Czech students did in January 1969.)
    Is it an appeal for unlimited freedom of speech or merely for the right to utter unpopular views? Consider questions 8 and 9 in the light of this utterance.

Chapter 3

Winning the right to vote

Ask almost anyone how long this country has been a democracy and he will reply 'for centuries'. In a sense this is true: there have nearly always been *some* democratic elements in our society. But it is only as recently as 1928 that every man and woman secured an equal right to vote, and only since 1948 that there has been 'one man, one vote'.

Since 1832 there has been a progressive widening of the franchise (the right to vote) and successively middle-class and working-class people have won that right. 'Won' is the correct term because each extension has followed a struggle by people who, up to that time, had been excluded. The exception is, perhaps, the granting of votes at eighteen in 1969. There was no evident demand for votes by the 18—21 year olds.

The Reform Act of 1832 is looked upon as a landmark — a break-through — yet it increased the proportion of voters only from 5 per cent to 10 per cent of the adult population. Substantially, it gave the vote to middle-class men who owned some property. Many working-class people who had joined the agitation for votes, those for example who had been in the thick of the Bristol riots and had their heads broken with those of other 'reformers', felt cheated. They organised themselves into a movement to secure the six aims of the People's Charter:

1. Universal adult (male) suffrage.
2. Secret voting.
3. Equal electoral districts.
4. Abolition of the property qualification for Members of Parliament.

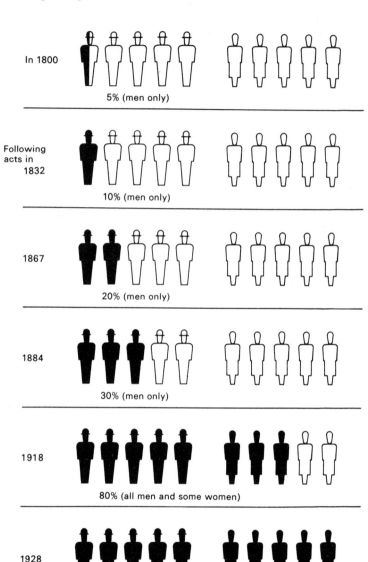

In 1800
5% (men only)

Following acts in 1832
10% (men only)

1867
20% (men only)

1884
30% (men only)

1918
80% (all men and some women)

1928
100% (all men and women)

(Percentages rounded up to next 5% in 1800, and 10% thereafter)
The numbers of voters rose from half a million in 1830 to over 35 million in 1965.
This is a faster rate than that shown and is due to the fact that the population (on which the percentages shown above were calculated) grew fast from 1800 to 1930.
Fig. 2 Proportion of adult population with the vote

5.   Payment of Members of Parliament.

6.   Annual Parliaments.

The Chartists, as these people were called, held meetings and demonstrations all over the country, getting people to sign a petition demanding reforms as set out in the Charter. The organisation embraced people of a wide range of opinion and formed a focus for agitation on issues other than those in the Charter. In the industrial North the vile conditions in the workhouses under the new Poor Law were exposed. One fiery clergyman, the Rev. J. R. Stevens, produced a horsewhip in the pulpit, declaring that it had been used in the local workhouse, and demanding that the people responsible should be hanged. Other Chartist leaders advocated monetary and land reform. Broadly, the movement had two wings, the 'moral force' group, mainly better-off artisans of London and the South, and the 'physical force' group from the harsher North and Wales. In Monmouthshire, in South Wales, the Chartists planned an armed revolt. Secretly, they assembled in the mining valleys and began to march on Newport, hoping to start a revolt that would gather strength as they advanced on London. In darkness and driving rain many of the marchers lost their way over the mountains. Those who reached Newport were met by rifle fire from the Militia, warned in advance, who ambushed them in Westgate Square. John Frost and other leaders were arrested, tried and sentenced to death, but after wide protests, reprieved and deported to Australia. Meanwhile the 'moral force' Chartists, who relied upon persuasion, organised meetings, published books, pamphlets and newspapers. Signatures were gathered for huge petitions to Parliament. The last, in 1848, was said to contain 6 million signatures, but when examined, had fewer than 2 million and contained many bogus signatures, such as 'Victoria Rex', 'The Duke of Wellington', 'Flintnose', 'Pugnose', many in the same handwriting. But though the movement ended in some derision, it had had its effect: despite the leadership of a number of cranks, half-crazy mob-orators and many worthy but not very effective people, it had won the support of millions of poor and exploited working-class folk who contributed their pennies and in whom it created a sense of hope: that, if the vote were theirs then Parliament would improve their conditions and make life more bearable. It had the support, too, of the better educated artisans and many rich radicals. In fact, all the aims — save one — have since been achieved.

3.1 Universal adult suffrage

In 1867 working men in the towns secured the vote; in 1884 it was extended to the countryside. Householders of all classes now had the vote; lodgers and the sons of householders were still without the vote, as were women.

Women's struggle for the vote is now well known. Like the Chartists, they had their peaceful persuaders and users of physical force. The latter broke windows, set fire to letterboxes and chained themselves to railings. In prison they went on hunger strike and were forcibly fed, a process described as torture by some who had suffered it. Miss Emily Davison ran on to the racecourse to stop the King's horse in the Derby of 1913 and was killed.

The 1914—18 war broke out while the agitation was at its height. The suffragettes called off the campaign and organised women for work in munition factories. This, it is said, greatly influenced many who had hitherto opposed votes for women. At least, it gave politicians an excuse for changing their minds and in 1918 the Representation of People Act gave votes to all men over twenty-one on a residential (no longer a property) qualification and to all women over thirty. The notion that women were only capable of exercising political discretion at thirty, while men were capable at twenty-one was subject to considerable ridicule and in 1928 an Act was passed giving women the vote at twenty-one in equality with men.

This might be thought to have given us a fully democratic franchise: but not quite. There were some people with more than one vote. Businessmen with premises away from their residence were entitled to an additional vote in the constituencies where their businesses were. For example, all the partners in the firm of Pidgeon, Pidgeon, O'Hara and Pidgeon, Solicitors — all eight of them — could have an extra vote by virtue of their one-room branch office in a neighbouring town. In certain constituencies, like the City of London, the business vote predominated, there being few other voters than a handful of shopkeepers and caretakers. These constituencies were predominantly Conservative. There were also the university constituencies, returning some twelve Members of Parliament (separate from the Members for the towns — such as Oxford — where the universities were situated). The electors were graduates. It was said that the university members were independent-minded and formed a useful leaven among the more orthodox party members: that accordingly they would introduce legislation on divorce and other controversial issues that the government was unwilling to touch.

All forms of plural voting, that is the businessmen's vote and the university vote, were abolished in 1948. Since then we have had 'one man, one vote'. Nevertheless, there are still plenty of Members willing to introduce controversial bills, witness Mr Abse's Bills on Divorce and Homosexuality, and Mr Steele's on Abortion.

An Act of Parliament giving votes at eighteen years of age received the Royal Assent on 17 April 1969. The Committee on the Age of Majority under the chairmanship of Mr Justice Latey, which did *not* consider the voting issue, had recommended that, in view of the fact that most young people today mature earlier than in the past, the age of full legal capacity should be lowered to eighteen. Following the implementation of this proposal on 1 January 1970, young people of eighteen were able to marry without the consent of parents, or the court (though the minimum age for marriage or 'consent' to sexual intercourse remained at sixteen); to enter into a contract; to hold land; to make a will; to be a blood-donor; to have his or her, own passport. It was in the light of these recommendations, that the government made its decision to reduce the voting age to eighteen.

3.2 Secret voting

Part 2 of the Charter was achieved by the Ballot Act of 1872. Before that Act, a voter went to the polling booth — outdoors — and declared his wish by word of mouth. Bystanders were present to jeer, or hustle, or report the decision to a voter's landlord or employer whose anger it was unwise to incur. William Cobbett (1763–1835), writing of his experiences at the polling booth, found that a heavy ring on the right hand helped him fight his way out of an angry crowd — usually paid toughs at the polling booth. Since 1872 we have been able to cast our vote in secret and be sure that no one will ever know for whom we voted, unless we choose to tell him.

3.3 Equal electoral districts

Equal electoral districts, necessary if each man's vote is to have the same weight, are not so easy to achieve. People *will* move. Thus, in the period between the wars Greater London doubled in size. People moved out from the crowded inner London boroughs to the new council and building society estates on the outskirts. The effect was to halve the number of voters in some of the older boroughs and quadruple the number in some of the newly built-up areas. If in one area there were 80,000 voters to choose one Member of Parliament, and 20,000 in another, then, at least theoretically, the influence of each voter in the second area was four times that in the former. The answer is found in the constant change of constituency boundaries, but this is a difficult political operation.

To say that ancient borough A and the neighbouring borough B shall no longer have one Member of Parliament each but shall be combined because only together do they have the required number of voters is to arouse wrath from thousands of citizens in both A and B. When a town has grown and has enough voters for two Members of Parliament, are all the citizens delighted? Yes, until actual proposals for its division are made. Perhaps it was a more than marginal Labour seat before: now it is to be divided into East and West. The East (the smoky industrial area) will be Labour and the West (the cleaner, more expensive area) Conservative. This is a net gain for the Conservatives and there will be complaints from Labour. Why not divide it into North and South? Both areas will then be marginal and neither party pleased.

In 1948 a Boundaries Commission was set up to make a continuous review of constituencies. It investigates, consults interests and reports and is building up a reputation for fairness. Its findings come before Parliament and changes are made by the decision of both Houses. By this process wholesale changes are avoided, as is the accusation that the party in power is 'gerrymandering',* that is, altering boundaries to favour its own electoral chances. In 1969 the Labour government was accused of gerrymandering by using its majority to vote down some of the recommendations of the Boundaries Commission brought before Parliament. It claimed:

1. That the alterations made did not necessarily favour its own chances.
2. That the constituencies omitted would shortly be the subject of local government boundary changes and it was desirable to wait until those changes were established before asking the Boundaries Commission to look at the question again.

One proposal to avoid even the appearance of gerrymandering is that the decisions of the Boundaries Commission should be applied without reference to Parliament, but Parliament is unlikely to allow these important decisions out of its own hands.

The country was divided into 630 areas, or constituencies, at the time of the 1970 general election, the aim being to have approximately 50,000 to 60,000 electors in each constituency. The largest was Billericay, in Essex, with 124,000, and the smallest, Birmingham, Ladywood, with just under 19,000. Some of the remote Scottish areas, such as Orkney and Zetland (26,000) and Western Isles (23,000), have smaller than average numbers, but it is agreed by all parties that a constituency of average size according to population there would be too big geographically for its Member to cover. If the recommendations

---

* A word coined from the name of Governor Gerry of Massachusetts who was accused of this practice.

of the Boundaries Commission are accepted there will be 635 constituencies at the general election following that of 1970.

3.4 Payment for Members of Parliament and abolition of property qualifications

One of the first points of the Charter to be secured was the abolition of the property qualification for Members of Parliament (1858). From that date a poor man could become a Member − if he could support himself − for there was no payment for the job. It was assumed that Members were persons of substance. When Labour Members were first elected they were either supported by the trade unions that sponsored them − particularly the miners − or by local political associations.

In 1909 a railwayman called Osborne, a member of the Amalgamated Society of Railway Servants, now the NUR, claimed that his union had no power to spend money on political purposes, though it had been doing so for years. The case went through the courts to the House of Lords which upheld his claim. Henceforth, until the law was changed, no union was able to pay its Members of Parliament, nor spend money on elections.

The Labour Members were in a fix in the general election of 1910 and begged and borrowed money to fight. They returned to Parliament clamouring for legislation to reverse the Osborne Judgement. The Liberal government got over the immediate problem by voting salaries for Members of Parliament and this has continued.

3.5 Annual Parliaments

The Chartists wanted each Parliament to last for one year only, so that the electors could get rid of an unwanted government in the ensuing general election. This is the only point in the Charter not achieved. We now have five-year Parliaments. A government may fall before the expiry of that time by losses in by-elections that imperil its majority, or by the break-up of the party supporting it. The Prime Minister decides when he will 'go to the country'; that is, have a general election. He chooses the time most favourable for his party. He considers not only the state of the economy and what it may be in a few months' time, but the weather (people will not turn out on a wet November evening) and holiday times − but he may not go beyond the five years.

It appears unlikely that the present length of Parliaments − five years − will be reduced. The opposition, naturally, is impatient that it cannot get the government out. But governments need time to put their policies into operation and await results. They must be able to introduce unpopular measures and still have time for the electors to get over their anger before the next election: otherwise unpopular measures will be shirked.

Of course, there is nothing magic in the term of five years: it might be four or six. In New Zealand it is three. What we have to balance are the greater responsiveness to the people's wish on the one hand and the need for stable government on the other.

3.6 The referendum

We have a general election every five years (at least) and that decides which party shall form the next government.

Some people argue that within the five-year term issues arise on which the opinion of the electorate has not been heard and on which it should be taken. For example, in the 1970 election both parties favoured entry to the European Economic Community if the terms then being negotiated were satisfactory. When the terms had been settled a number of people said that on such an important issue 'reference' should be made to the electorate, that is, a vote be taken on whether or not the electors thought the terms acceptable. Such a vote is termed a 'Referendum'.

Opponents of the referendum said that it was unnecessary and unsuitable — unnecessary because we elect Members of Parliament to decide such technical and detailed matters and unsuitable because it would not be possible to phrase the questions so as to produce a plain 'Yes' or 'No' answer which is all that a referendum can provide. Members of Parliament, it is argued, who are chosen by the people, are more knowledgeable and more politically experienced than the average voter and less likely to be swayed by specious arguments and prejudice. Many reforms, it was said, such as the introduction of compulsory education, religious tolerance, the abolition of the death penalty, would probably not have been adopted if put to the popular vote.

Advocates of a referendum, returning to the EEC issue argued that it was not a mere matter of terms: it was about a basic constitutional issue — where political decisions affecting Britain should be taken, in Westminster or in Europe. A referendum had not proved impracticable in other countries: Eire, Norway and Denmark had voted on entry to the EEC. The people of Eire and Denmark said 'Yes' and the people of Norway 'No'. In some countries, such as Switzerland, the referendum had been used more frequently: in 1959 the electorate had said 'No' to the granting of votes to women but reversed that decision in 1971.

There is, it is conceded, a case for the use of the referendum on local issues. Thus, the Welsh towns voted for or against the Sunday opening of pubs in 1961. There was a referendum in Northern Ireland on the border issue in 1973.

Usually it is the opposition that suggests taking a referendum: having failed to get its way in Parliament, it sees it as a second line of attack. Those in power tend to argue for the supremacy of Parliament — hence the spectacle of the same politician advocating its use on one occasion and opposing it on another.

We must now consider 'the appeal to the electorate': just how a general election works.

Questions *for discussion and action*
1. The late Sir Alan Herbert, one of the last university MPs, suggested the reintroduction of university constituencies, say twenty seats shared among the forty universities: graduates and third-year undergraduates to have a vote and say, half the candidates to be under thirty years of age and to resign on reaching thirty. This would provide 'twenty voices with not merely the right to speak but a duty to answer for the universities, if there are any complaints'.

   It would, said Sir Alan, give an opportunity for youth's demand for 'participation', provide an outlet for energy now wasted on futile demonstrations and provide a reason for students to go to Westminster for the redress of grievances. (*The Times*, 24 January 1969).

   Discuss this proposal for the reintroduction of plural voting.
2. Are there any other qualifications (e.g. headship of a family, business responsibility, possession of a knowledge of politics) that would warrant the granting of an extra vote?
3. Should there be an educational test for prospective voters? If so, should it include all or any of the following:
   (a) A literacy test indicating the ability to read and write.
   (b) Ability to name the constituency and its MP.
   (c) Ability to name the main functions of local government.
   (d) Ability to name the main function of central government.
   (e) Ability to distinguish the main taxes such as income tax and VAT and state on what commodities Customs and Excise taxes are levied (such as petrol, beer and tobacco).

   (To avoid upsetting existing electors these tests could be applied perhaps to new voters at eighteen, immigrants and naturalised British subjects.)
4. Do you think that reducing the voting age to eighteen has led to a greater or lesser interest in politics among the younger voters? In

what ways is that interest shown? How could it be developed?

Prepare a questionnaire to test your opinion on this question, and ask your colleagues (and any others of the age-group involved) to complete it. Collate the information obtained and discuss with colleagues the accuracy of your original opinions.

Chapter 4

A general election

Under our constitution we must have a general election at least once every five years.

Having decided when he wishes to have his general election, the Prime Minister goes to the Queen and asks for the dissolution of Parliament. This she grants. Voting day is fixed — generally on a Thursday — some three weeks after dissolution. When Parliament is dissolved Members cease to be Members but the government, that is the Queen's Ministers, remain in office to carry on the day-to-day business of government.

4.1 The candidates

In each constituency the parties now decide who shall be their standard bearer. In most cases this is a formality, the decision having been made months before. The sitting Member is usually the candidate for *his* party if he wishes to continue. He has the advantage of being well known and has probably impressed himself upon the electors as a hard-working constituency man: he has been seen at public functions, has supported charitable bazaars and garden parties and, above all, attended to the personal problems of many hundreds of his constituents. Most Members of Parliament have a heavy correspondence on such matters and in addition hold a 'surgery' on, say, alternate Friday evenings in their constituencies when, with a local councillor and a friendly solicitor or social worker, they are available for consultation. The opposition parties, also, will probably have chosen their 'prospective'

Parliamentary candidates many months before. They too, will have made themselves known to the electors, by speeches, by writing letters to the local newspapers and by participation in as many local functions as they can.

4.2 Nomination

Party meetings are now called and the candidates are formally 'adopted' and nomination procedure starts. Each candidate appoints an agent (probably the paid full-time local agent of his party) who is responsible for the campaign and whose duty it is to see that the nomination is properly carried out, that the campaign literature is issued in the proper form and that expenditure is kept within the limits set down by law. Any infringement of law, for example, the treating of voters to drinks or other bribery, spending of more than the permitted amount, the failure to submit accounts in the prescribed detail and form, and by the prescribed date, may result in an elected member being unseated.

Nomination is, literally, 'naming' the candidate to the returning officer (frequently the local Town Clerk or in country areas, the Clerk of the County Council). Five voters in the constituency have to sign the nomination paper in the presence of a Justice of the Peace. The agent, to be on the safe side in case there is a technical error in the first paper, will take along two or three completed nomination papers. In some places it is the custom to take along a fistful — several from each 'ward' or local polling area — as a propaganda gesture — as to say, 'look what a lot of support our man has'.

Nominations have to be in by an appointed day and the deposit of £150 paid in cash. (The deposit will be forfeited if the candidate gets less than one-eighth of the votes cast.) Who can be a candidate? Practically anyone over twenty-one qualified to vote, that is, a British citizen having a residential qualification — not necessarily in the constituency where he stands. The three main exceptions are criminals, lunatics and Members of the House of Lords. The reason for the exclusion of the first two is obvious; the third is already a Member of Parliament — for Parliament includes the Lords as well as the Commons. Accordingly, he may not sit in the Commons as well.

When nominations are complete, the local campaign begins.

4.3 The campaign

The national campaign has been swinging for some time. Many of the last acts of the government have been directed at the electors. Speeches by the party leaders in the country and on the radio and television have been the opening shots in the campaign. The parties have long prepared their manifestos, the result of years of debate throughout the party and anxious discussion by the party leaders who have struggled to produce a statement that will:

(1)   Appeal to a wide section of the voters, especially the non-party voters;

(2)   Enthuse their active members;

(3)   Form a practical basis for the next session when, they hope, they will be in charge of the nation's affairs.

Party policies will be discussed in detail later, but it will be seen at once that to satisfy points (1) and (2) will be a difficult job, for the active members are frequently those with the strongest and most extreme views, whereas the non-party voters, the so-called 'floating voters', are likely to be frightened by any extreme declaration of policy. Satisfying the third point is a long-term insurance: for if the party, as government, does not do what it has promised, its supporters will become disillusioned. What *can* be done in any situation is sufficiently circumscribed to cause disillusion anyhow: parties are therefore wise not to promise too much.

Newspapers give publicity to the party manifestos, publishing them in full or in summary with appropriate comment. The Prime Minister and some of his most popular colleagues are touring the areas where their support lies, making important speeches, outlining the policy the party will pursue if returned to government. Opposition leaders have similar tours planned by their central offices. At party headquarters in London there are daily 'press conferences' where newspaper correspondents get the latest news from the parties' campaign managers. Each side is looking for weaknesses in its opponent's case: each hoping that a gaff by one of its leading opponents will give an opening for attack. Has the other side promised too much? Has a leading figure lost his temper under 'heckling' — that is, from questions or interjections shouted at him while he is speaking, perhaps on a wet and windy day out of doors? If so, it will be highlighted by his opponents and conclusions drawn, often far beyond what is warranted. Of course, some politicians thrive under heckling and turn it to advantage. All aspects of policy are brought out and reactions watched. If a topic sparks off headlines in the press or on television, there will be an attempt to build it up into an 'issue'. Thus, during the campaign a number of issues will emerge and the main debate will be concentrated upon them. Almost certainly these will concern home and not foreign affairs: pensions, taxation, incomes policy, comprehensive or selective education. If the party in office thinks it has done a good job and is in the lead it will plump for a quiet election and rely on its record. Then the opposition sets the pace and tries to 'force' the issues, as in 1970, when the Conservatives highlighted rising prices and swept in with promises to halt inflation and cut taxation.

The local campaign will be a reflection of the national campaign: the candidates issue their addresses, based on the party manifestos but with a local bias wherever possible. There will be photographs of the candidate, if possible with his wife and family, and a brief biography. If the Labour candidate went to Eton it will not be mentioned ('What does it matter where he was educated!') If the Conservative is a trade unionist it will certainly be mentioned.

Active party members will be pressed into canvassing, that is, calling from door to door, to ask people on the electoral list if they will vote for the candidate their party is putting up. Some people object to telling canvassers how they are intending to vote on the grounds that the ballot is secret. Some people are annoyed if they are *not* canvassed and complain of neglect. There is usually very little political discussion involved as the main object of the party workers is to find who are their supporters, so that they can be 'pulled out' on polling night, if they have not voted during the day. Provided the canvasser is polite, he will usually be received courteously.

Other party members will be busy addressing envelopes to take the party message to voters; young members will be delivering them door to door. At a general election the parties are allowed one free postal delivery to each voter. These contain the election address and exhortations to supporters to work, subscribe to party funds and, of course, to turn out and vote. Posters appear on the hoardings on sites booked long in advance. Bills appear in windows indicating support for one party or another, emphasising simply the candidate's name and associating it with his party. There is local rivalry to get more bills up in the street than the other party. The more enthusiastic members go in for illicit fly-posting or painting slogans on strategic walls. There is defacement and counter-defacement. The police usually turn a blind eye to much of this (mildly illegal) activity which is considered a part of the election game. There are local public meetings, which at one time were thought to be dying out, but in recent years have regained popularity especially if nationally known speakers are included. There may be 'motorcades', processions of cars through busy shopping areas on the Saturday before polling day. There are loud-speaker vans patrolling the streets and street corner meetings.

4.4 Polling day

By polling day the agents on both sides will have collated the lists

1	**CROFT**	
	Norman Eric 3 The Knolls, Kirkella Hertfordshire LABOUR	
2	**LARKIN**	
	Colin Spencer 27 Mill Street, Kirkella Hertfordshire LIBERAL	
3	**OWENS**	
	John Terence 42 Gable End Villas, Kirkella Hertfordshire CONSERVATIVE	

Ballot paper

brought in by canvassers, and have a fair idea of the support they may expect. Their efforts are now concentrated on 'getting the voters out'. The national radio and television campaign has come to an end, but the news bulletins from early morning on polling day remind the voters throughout the day of their duty to vote. The newspapers contain last-minute appeals from the party leaders and exhortations to readers not to neglect their electoral duties. The loud-speaker vans are out and a steady stream of voters makes its way to the local polling stations in schools and public libraries. Outside the polling stations no party posters may be placed but representatives of the parties stand there to show the flag and to take the registration numbers of people who vote (though, of course, not to ask *how* they voted). This information is sent back to the committee rooms and checked off with the list of supporters. As the day proceeds calls are made on supporters who have not yet voted: perhaps a lift by car is offered. Efforts to bring out supporters who have not yet voted are intensified as the evening proceeds, supporters are called upon again, party workers become more persuasive, cars dash to and from the polling stations.

If it pours with rain in the evening, the Labour people are worried, and the Conservatives not too displeased, for the bulk of Labour supporters turn out (or do not turn out) in the evening when they get home from work whereas many Conservatives are able to vote in the daytime.

At 10 o'clock the policeman at the door of the polling station looks to see if there are any last-minute voters on the way, lets them in under his arm and closes the door. When the last voter has been issued with his ballot paper, put his cross against the person of his choice, folded it and dropped it into the ballot box, the official in charge of the station closes and seals the boxes and they are taken under police escort to the town or county hall. Here the count takes place, a process now made familiar by television. The returning officer is in charge, aided by the town hall staff. The party agents are there to see fair play, supported by scrutineers from among the party workers. Later the candidates and their wives arrive, trying to look unconcerned.

By now, most of the active workers are resting their feet at home or in the 'local', their eyes on the television where commentators fill out by background comment the time before the first declarations are expected (about midnight). Literally millions of people stay up into the small hours to hear the result of their local election and to guess at the final result — just a few hours earlier than they would know if they went to bed and waited for the morning papers: for the contest is now at the cup-tie stage with a good bit invested — in expectations and fears if not in money — on the result.

Questions *for discussion and action*

1. Party candidates are often selected at party meetings attended by the committee members only: say twenty to forty people. In a 'safe' seat they are actually choosing the Member of Parliament. Can you suggest ways in which more people would be involved?
2. Does the fact that each candidate for Parliament has to make a deposit of £150 prevent ordinary people from standing? It is said to discourage 'frivolous candidatures'. Is this the case?
3. Should candidates have to pass a test of intellectual and moral

fitness? This was suggested by some Chartists in 1856 who wanted a 'higher intellectual and moral standard' among Members of Parliament [1].

4. Does 'canvassing' infringe the secrecy of the ballot?
5. If you were canvassing for your party what would you say to people who said:
   (a) I vote as my husband says.
   (b) I don't believe in politics.
   (c) How I vote can't make any difference.
ᴑ. Consider the following opinion given by a student on the use of 'motorcades' at a general election:

> When I saw the Conservative motorcade going through the streets of Hampstead I wondered what I was supposed to think: that the Conservatives are well off? (and I can't afford one). Or that because they have cars they will govern the country better than Labour? Or that there are a lot of them? The last idea doesn't impress me. When I saw the Labour motorcade what did I think? That 'we' also have cars? Or that Labour is now respectably middle class? Or that there are a lot us, too? When I saw the Hampstead Communist motorcade I laughed. They were a tatty lot. Workers? (Teachers, I expect.) Driving on with red flags to the revolution? (Not today, comrades, its raining.) One thing in their favour — some of them did look shamefaced. Forward with the snobs.

In your opinion:
   (a) Has the motorcade any value unnoticed by the writer?
   (b) Do you agree with her reactions?
   (c) Does a motorcade make a reasonable or unreasonable appeal? If unreasonable, would you urge the parties to discontinue the practice?
7. While we may vote at eighteen years of age, we may not stand as a candidate for Parliament until twenty-one.
   Do you think that we should be allowed to stand for Parliament at eighteen?
8. If an election is pending in your constituency or a general election is in prospect, conduct an election on similar lines in your school or college.

Chapter 5

Forming an administration

5.1 After the election: who has won?

The votes are counted in most of the big towns and cities on the evening of polling day. In the county constituencies the count usually starts next morning and most of the results are out by early afternoon. It is now clear which party has won the election.

That phrase needs some explanation. In each constituency the candidate with the most votes is declared the Member of Parliament and the party with the largest number of MPs throughout the country is said to have won. This produces some anomalies. If there are more than two candidates in a constituency the member may have got in on a minority vote. Thus in 1970 the result at Brecon and Radnor was:

Labour	18,736
Conservative	13,892
Liberal	8,169
Welsh Nat.	2,349
Labour majority	4,844

The Labour man was in with 18,700 votes, although there were 24,000 votes against him.

In some areas, for example coal-mining constituencies, the Labour candidate usually gets in with a huge majority. At Hemsworth (West Yorkshire), in 1970, the result was:

Labour	40,013
Conservative	9,534
Labour majority	30,479

On the other hand, agricultural and seaside areas with a large number of elderly, retired people return Conservative members with a big majority. At Rye, Sussex, in 1970 the result was:

Conservative	32,300
Labour	9,031
Liberal	8,947
Conservative majority	23,269

As a result of these differences, it may well be that the party with the most votes throughout the country is not the party with the most Members of Parliament. In 1951 the final figures at the general election showed:

Party	Votes (per cent of votes)		MPs	Per cent of members
Labour	13,949,000	(48.8)	295	47.2
Conservative	13,718,000	(48.0)	321	51
Liberal	731,000	(2.5)	6	1
Others	200,000	(0.7)	3	0.5

It will be seen that the Labour Party won more votes than the Conservatives but fewer seats. The Conservatives were held to have won and formed the government. The reason is that the contest is for power in the House of Commons. The aim of each party is to get a clear majority of Members of Parliament over the other parties combined. If it does, it can 'govern', that is, it can get its Bills through on a vote in the House of Commons, including the all-important finance Bills which put into effect the provisions of the Budget. Without this majority it is at the mercy of the other parties and can pass only what they approve. It *may* consider that this is the best thing to do as the Labour Party did in 1924 and 1929 when it took office as a minority government, that is, without enough Members to get its Bills through, except with the support of the Liberals. It was the first time that the Labour Party had formed a government and did so to show that it was 'fit to govern', that is, that it had sufficient good men to fill all the jobs and conduct the affairs of the nation. It fell when the Liberals voted against it.

In recent years general elections have given the Labour Party or the Conservatives a majority of Members, sometimes too narrow to be comfortable (as the Labour majority of six in 1964) but sufficient to enable the Government to carry on. But the Liberal Party has come off badly, getting a smaller percentage of MPs than its share of votes warrants. (See 1951 result p. 39).

5.2 The new Prime Minister

To return to the day following polling day: if the party that was in before the election, wins, the leader of that party, who is still Prime Minister, will go to the Queen with the resignations of his colleagues and be commissioned to form a new government. If he has lost the election he will give the Queen his resignation. She will thank him for his services, then call the leader of the successful party to the Palace. He will be invited to form a government and go off to consult his colleagues. He will, of course, already have given much anxious thought to this question. By tradition, he has forty-eight hours in which to fill the main ministerial posts. He will submit the names of his team to the Queen for acceptance, they in turn will go to Buckingham Palace and 'kiss hands', and receive the seals of office, and the new administration is formed.

5.3 The new administration

The Prime Minister has about 100 offices to fill. These form the 'Government' who administer the affairs of State, and govern so long as they have the support of the rest of the party in Parliament. The most important Ministers comprise the Cabinet, an inner group that meets regularly at the Prime Minister's residence, 10 Downing Street, off Whitehall, and makes the most important government decisions.

(a) The Cabinet
The number of Ministers in the Cabinet and its composition depends upon the Prime Minister. It has been the practice to have a small Cabinet in war-time but a larger one in peace-time. The number of Members varies from twelve to twenty-three or twenty-four. The holders of certain important offices are invariably in the Cabinet. These include the Chancellor of the Exchequer, who presides over the department known as the Treasury and is responsible for raising and spending the vast sums needed to run a modern State; the Home Secretary, in charge of the Home Office which supervises home security, the police and prisons; the Foreign Secretary, in charge of our relations with other countries, including Commonwealth countries; the Secretary of State

for Defence, in charge of the three armed services, Army, Navy and Air Force; and the Lord Chancellor, who is an eminent lawyer and president (or chairman) of the House of Lords.

Ministers in charge of other departments could not all be in the Cabinet without making it too big for efficient working. Hence, only departments held to be of special importance are represented. In the Conservative Administration formed after the general election of 1970 Trade and Industry, Employment, the Social Services, Education and Science, Agriculture Fisheries and Food, the Environment, Wales and Scotland were included. In addition there were two Ministers with honorific titles but few, if any, departmental duties, the Lord President of the Council (that is of the Privy or Private, Council of the Queen) and the Lord Privy Seal (custodian of the Great Seal of England), who are leaders of the House of Commons and House of Lords respectively. They manage the day-to-day business there, consulting with their counterparts in the opposition, to ensure the efficient flow of business.

(b) Ministers outside the Cabinet
Outside the Cabinet (in 1970) were Ministers in charge of Transport, Housing and Construction, Aviation, the Post Office, Overseas Development; assistant Ministers (often called Ministers of State) at the busiest offices, such as the Home and Foreign Offices and the Treasury; the Law Officers, namely, the Attorney General, the Lord Advocate (Scotland) and the Solicitor General; and a great number of Under Secretaries and Parliamentary Secretaries who assist in the various departments. Finally, there are the Whips — a title which is a hang-over from the days when Members of Parliament were mainly country gentlemen given to hunting. The Whips see to the day-to-day business of the House and ensure that Members are present in force when important debates are held and votes to be taken: stray Members, like stray hounds, will be whipped into the pack when need arises.

(c) The art of forming a government
The Prime Minister's task in forming a government and deciding who shall be in the Cabinet is a difficult one. He has to choose the most able people in his party mainly, but not exclusively, from Members of the House of Commons or the House of Lords. If he brings in an outsider (as Mr Churchill brought in Mr Bevin the trade union leader in 1940, and Mr Heath brought in Mr John Davies the businessman in 1970) a seat in the House of Commons must be found for him within a reasonable time. One way is to get an older member to resign from a safe seat so that a by-election may be held with the Minister as candidate. Or the Minister may be created a Life Peer and so have a seat in the Lords. A

number of Ministers must be in the Lords as government business has to be conducted there, as well as in the Commons.

In a predominantly two-party system, it is inevitable that there will be a wide spread of opinion in each of the two main parties: in a sense, each party is a coalition, that is, a coming together of people with differing views but with a measure of agreement on the main issues. A Prime Minister, in choosing his administration, will have to ensure that all important views are represented and interests balanced. Personal rivalries among his Ministers must be borne in mind. (Mr Attlee, in 1945, was said to have put Mr Bevin at the Foreign Office and Mr Morrison in charge of Home Affairs so that they would not come into too close contact.) Personal ambition must be taken into account. Mr X may not accept the office of Minister of Posts and Telecommunications because he has already held higher office. But the election has brought in abler men and there is no higher post available. Mr Y was not a success last time and is to be dropped. Mr Z is an extremist whom it would be unwise to leave without office and with nothing to do but lead revolts. The Prime Minister will be tempted to give him a heavy department and hope that office will draw his sting.

(d) The work of the Cabinet

The Prime Minister presides over the Cabinet, guides its discussions and leads it to decisions. After a general election it will need first to decide which items of policy are to be given priority. All important political decisions are made in Cabinet and otherwise unresolved disputes between departments are settled there. Lesser decisions, but of course, in total, the great majority, are made in the various departments. The Cabinet is thus the controlling committee of the government. Because its Members are very heavily pressed, many with large departments of State to supervise, the Cabinet delegates much of its work to committees. It expects these committees and individual Ministers to submit issues to it in concise memoranda, with the main arguments clearly set out. Cabinet Ministers not only need to be men of intelligence and wide experience, but to have that indefinable quality 'judgement'; the ability to sum up a situation, seize its essentials, be sensitive to its implications and above all be able to make firm decisions.

A Minister is responsible for the actions of his department. If one of his officials makes a mistake, he must take the blame. No civil servant will wish to bring discredit on his department and expose his Minister to public embarrassment, hence the care with which decisions are made. The citizen whose case is being considered may think the delay is unnecessary and the whole procedure inefficient. It is often no more than the price of 'accountability'. When any mistake may well be exposed in Parliament or the papers, the result is bound to be excessive caution.

The Cabinet works on the principle of collective responsibility. Once a decision has been taken all must stand by it. If a Minister cannot do so he must resign. Of course, he may remain quiet, stay within the Cabinet and 'live to fight another day'. All Cabinet discussions are confidential and may not be disclosed. Ministers may thus be completely frank and the argument pursued until a practical decision is reached. Then, as noted, all must accept or go.

(e) The qualities of a Prime Minister

A Prime Minister requires very special qualities. His position has changed over the years. There was a time when the king presided over the meetings with his Ministers. But George I rarely attended Cabinet meetings because he could not understand English and English affairs bored him. Naturally someone had to step into the leadership. That person became known as the 'Prime Minister' and at first this was a term of abuse. Sir Robert Walpole, who was First Lord of the Treasury from 1721 to 1742, refused to acknowledge the name although he was in fact the leading figure among the Ministers. Since then the party system has developed and the Prime Minister depends on party support rather than on that of his friends as in Walpole's day. Indeed (as noted), it is now the constitutional practice for the Queen to invite the leader of the successful party at a general election to become Prime Minister. Traditionally, the Prime Minister is the Queen's adviser and keeps her in touch with affairs by regular communication.

The Prime Minister leads the government. He selects the Ministers and can dismiss them. He takes the chair at Cabinet meetings and has the last word in their deliberations. He is thus in a very powerful position. At the same time he is by no means a dictator. He has to keep his Cabinet together. This will not be easy because politicians are often people with strong wills and fixed ideas, individualistic and ambitious. (They have to be to make their way up in the party hierarchy.) It will not be easy to get them to work as a team. The Prime Minister's authority rests partly on his power to dismiss them, but mainly on his ability to carry them with him on a course that will be acceptable to the majority and not outrage the minority. They all know that the one thing they must avoid is to split the party. If the party in the House splits, its majority vanishes and it cannot survive. If the party in the country splits it cannot hope to win the confidence of the electors at the next election. And because all parties in this country are coalitions, the danger of fragmentation is always present. The successful leader is the one who knows instinctively what his party, in the House and in the country, will take.

Newspapers are now demanding that the Prime Minister shall be a 'professional'. Actually, the British system is built on the assumption that Ministers are amateurs and the civil servants professional, with the amateurs controlling the professionals. At one time the king's Ministers were important people called on by the king to supervise his affairs: they ministered, or managed them, as they managed their own estates, through their appointees, the civil servants, many of whom went in or out with a government. Since the 1850s recruitment to the Civil Service has been by examination, appointments are permanent and a professional Civil Service has grown up.

A professional Prime Minister, presumably, is one who has made a life-time's study of government and politics and knows how it works; has control of his administration; knows what is going on in all departments, yet does not interfere in day-to-day affairs; has mastery in the Commons and is not continually at the mercy of the opposition; keeps his party together in the House and the country and finally, in times of crisis, projects himself not just as the leader of a party but as the nation's leader.

This is a difficult prescription and few Prime Ministers have fulfilled it completely. But the Parliamentary system is a rigorous one and does seem to throw up men who are able to meet the needs of the occasion, various as these are. Politics is a matter of personalities as well as of policies and readers will find the study of past Prime Ministers and other politicians a fascinating one.

5.4 The Civil Service

The requirements of a civil servant are different from those of a Minister. A civil servant makes administrative decisions, a Minister political decisions. This distinction is, no doubt, an oversimplification, because the higher ranks of the Civil Service frequently have to make decisions having a political content. They do so in terms of 'what the Minister would have done'. It is important that Ministers should not be over-burdened with detail and the principal civil servants take much of the load.

Some people assert that our professional Civil Service has become too powerful and that too many decisions are taken by them. Much will depend on the strength of mind and will of the individual Minister: some Ministers control their civil servants; some are 'run' by them. Undoubtedly, civil servants, especially those in the top ranks, men of special intelligence and force, having the advantage of continuous service in a department (against the temporary occupation of the Minister) are in a powerful position. However, there is a strong tradition that the Civil Service is strictly non-political and is there to serve Ministers of whatever party.

Scepticism is voiced by those who note that the upper ranks are enlisted from a narrow range of upper-class candidates coming from Oxford and Cambridge Universities who form a close association by membership of exclusive West End clubs, where they meet to exchange views and plan strategy, not necessarily that desired by the Ministers. As one reads their biographies one can see that they are, indeed, able to influence policy: sometimes beneficially, when they prevent rash or unconsidered policies from being adopted.

Two suggestions have been made to counter any undesirable influence they may have: the first is to recruit from a wider social strata; the second that Ministers should bring with them expert advisers from their own parties who can balance the expertise of the civil servants.

Another criticism of the Civil Service is that it has too much power under 'delegated legislation', that is under laws that leave a great number of detailed decisions to Ministers — in reality to civil servants who deal with individual cases. Parliament has established a number of procedures to enable a citizen to appeal against unjust decisions by a civil servant. These are outlined in Chapter 9, which deals with the redress of grievances.

Questions *for discussion and action*

1. Under existing practice it is the party with the largest number of MPs, not necessarily with the most votes, that forms the government. Consider the case of 1951 (p. 39) and the following proposed methods of 'Proportional Representation'.

    (a) The Party List method, whereby each party would produce a list with the candidates in order of priority: each party would be allocated its proportionate number of MPs according to the total vote and they would be taken from the list irrespective of the number of votes cast for them in their locality.

    (b) The Alternative Vote method. Here the electors would vote for their first and second choice. If no candidate has an absolute majority of first choice votes, all candidates after the first two would fall out and the 'second choices' of the people that voted for them would be distributed among the first two;

      thus:

FIRST COUNT		SECOND COUNT	
First choice:		*'Second choice' votes of eliminated candidate distributed thus:*	*Total of First and Second choice votes:*
CONSERVATIVE	6,000	+ 500 =	6,500
LABOUR	5,000	+ 3,500 =	8,500
LIBERAL	4,000		

No candidate has absolute majority. 'Second choice' votes of third candidate distributed among the first two.

The Labour candidate, though second on the first count, wins on the second count.

(N.B. There are many other, more complicated systems, in use.)

What are the advantages and disadvantages of these methods?

2. Some people maintain that Proportional Representation, though arithmetically more democratic, would lead to *(a)* governments with very narrow majorities and/or *(b)* the balance lying with the third party.

Consider whether this would be better or worse than the existing situation.

3. Give a brief talk to your group on any political leader about whom you have read.

What, do you think, led him into political life?

What were his principal achievements?

What did his opponents think of him?

Chapter 6

Hereditary elements in Parliament

6.1 'The Queen in Parliament'

So far, we have spoken almost entirely of the House of Commons, mentioned the Lords briefly, and brought in the Queen as a passing reference. Constitutionally speaking, we are governed by 'The Queen in Parliament'.

The Norman kings called the wise men (that is the powerful men, the Barons) for a parley. Later, to offset the power of the barons, the king invited two knights from each shire (county) and two burgesses from each borough (town). These knights and burgesses, representing the 'Commons', met in a separate place from the king and his lords. They debated among themselves and agreed on the demands they would make on the king in return for the money he would require from them. The two Houses — Lords and Commons — remain separate to this day, and the whole government process continues to be known as 'The King (or Queen) in Parliament'.

6.2 The House of Lords

Since the early days of Parliament and particularly during the last century, the power of the Lords has declined and the power of the Commons, the elected body, has increased. At present the Lords cannot interfere with money matters: taxation is wholly in the hands of the Commons. This was achieved by the Parliament Act of 1911, a reaction to the Lords' refusal to pass Mr Lloyd George's Budget of 1909, which provided for Old Age Pensions and foreshadowed National Insurance; the beginning of what is now called the Welfare State. In 1949 the powers of the Lords were again cut down, because of their opposition to the Labour government's Steel Nationalisation Bill and now they can delay legislation for one year only and not three years as formerly.

The difficulty with the House of Lords is that its hereditary Members (sons of peers and sons of sons, etc.), totalling about 850, are overwhelmingly Conservative and can, if they wish, seriously delay legislation brought in by a Labour or Liberal government. Fortunately, they rarely attend. The continuance of the Lords may thus be said (facetiously, perhaps) to depend on the absenteeism of its Members [1].

Present-day governments may now ask the Queen to create 'Life Peers', appointed, as their title suggests, for one lifetime only. It enables any government to put supporters in the House of Lords to ensure that its business is effectively carried through there.

The Lords do useful work in looking again at legislation and regulations passed by the Commons. They can save the time of the Commons by initiating Bills and can hold valuable debates on topics where the varied experience of its Members, especially those recently created for distinguished service in industry, the professions or on foreign service, produces a high level of discussion. The Lords can speak more freely than Members of the House of Commons who have to be careful not to upset important sections of their constituents. This is especially the case where questions of divorce and sexual behaviour are at issue. The value of the Lords as a revising and deliberative chamber is now widely accepted and discussion concentrates on two questions regarding its membership: should the hereditary principle be abolished and from whom should the life Members be recruited?

6.3 The Sovereign

The British Sovereign is a constitutional monarch. Though the powers of our sovereigns have been reduced substantially over the years the reigning monarch retains some personal initiatives that may be exercised without reference to Parliament and all acts of government are still carried out in the Sovereign's name: for example, criminal proceedings are initiated in her name, and the chief appointments of State made similarly. However, her main prerogatives, or rights, are exercised almost entirely on her behalf by Ministers in Parliament. She thus appoints and dismisses Members of the Cabinet on the advice of the Prime Minister. She dissolves Parliament and summons a new one on

The State Opening of Parliament

that same advice. Even the 'Queen's Speech' with which a new Parliament opens although delivered by the Queen in the colourful setting of the House of Lords and with due ceremony, is the product of the government; an outline of its policy for the ensuing session. She never withholds her consent to properly enacted Bills of Parliament.

The Sovereign performs a useful function in providing continuity between administrations: in naming the new Prime Minister when the defeated one resigns. On most occasions there is no decision to make because the successful party at a general election has its established leader. But when a Prime Minister dies, or resigns through illness, or when the party splits, the Queen has a difficult political decision to make. In these circumstances she takes advice from experienced political leaders and invites the person whom she thinks to be most acceptable to form an administration. Otherwise her powers are confined to being consulted, to advise and warn. A sovereign with long experience of Parliaments and Prime Ministers may be able to sense the mood of the nation and give valuable advice. Since Queen Victoria's reign there has been no interference with the Prime Minister in his choice of Ministers. It is said that King George VI advised Mr Attlee to put Mr Ernest Bevin at the Foreign Office and not at the Treasury in 1945, but there is no evidence that this influenced Mr Attlee's decision. The Queen's main function is to endow State occasions with dignity and to encourage people in their good works by visits to hospitals, schools, youth clubs and work places. She is 'the fount of honours' and although the decisions are made by the Prime Minister and his advisers, the conferment of honours is graced by the Queen's presence. Equally, her State visits to open a new Parliament and the reading of the Queen's Speech, outlining the government's proposals for the new session, add dignity to the occasion, in the eyes of many people and impress on people at large the importance of Parliament.

There are many traditional Parliamentary ceremonies associated with the Queen's role as Head of the Government. When the Queen wishes to announce a decision her commissioners appear in the House of Lords and a messenger summons Members of the House of Commons to the Bar of the House of Lords. This was, until recently, a disturbing interference in the conduct of business in the Commons and agreement has been reached to limit it to convenient times. The door of the Commons is traditionally slammed in the face of Black Rod, the Queen's messenger, to keep afresh in people's minds the right of the Commons to bar the sovereign and to symbolise the supremacy of Parliament.

Questions *for discussion and action*

1. Consider whether the House of Lords should:
   - *(a)* Be abolished as undemocratic, in that its Members are mainly hereditary, i.e. there by 'right of birth';
   - *(b)* Be changed so that its Members are all elected like Members of the House of Commons. (The American 'second chamber', the Senate, is elected.)
   - *(c)* Be changed so that all its Members are appointed (e.g. as life peers) on the advice of the government so as to continue as a 'revising' and 'deliberative' second chamber.
2. Collect reports from the newspapers over a period showing the Queen performing her official duties. Give your opinion of their value. Honours are conferred in the name of the Queen. Consider whether or not you think this practice a desirable one. Note recent changes in the type of recipient — for example, sportsmen and women. Are there any people whom you think should receive them who do not do so at present?

Chapter 7

Parliament at work

7.1 Checks on power

We put very great powers into the hands of the government. The Prime Minister is supreme in the Cabinet. The Ministers are supported by highly organised and efficient government departments. The government has a majority in the Commons and can get its way.

How do we ensure that this concentration of power is not abused?

We have already seen that a government has to 'renew its mandate' every five years. We have seen, too, that the Prime Minister, despite his acknowledged power, is dependent on Cabinet colleagues, themselves men of considerable ability and independence. The government itself is dependent on its supporting party in Parliament, which in turn is dependent on the party in the country. These all provide limits to what the government can in fact do. There are, in addition, many checks on their power which arise out of the day-to-day operation of Parliament.

First, the government has to justify its acts before a highly critical audience in the House of Commons and the Lords. Its performance is reported in the newspapers and on radio and television. Every Bill it brings forward is debated extensively before it becomes law. Questions probing the government's efficiency are asked by Members from all sides of the House, but particularly by the opposition (see below), one of whose main functions is to keep the government on its toes. The proceedings of Parliament are published daily in *Hansard*, which gives a complete account of every word spoken in Parliament and is available

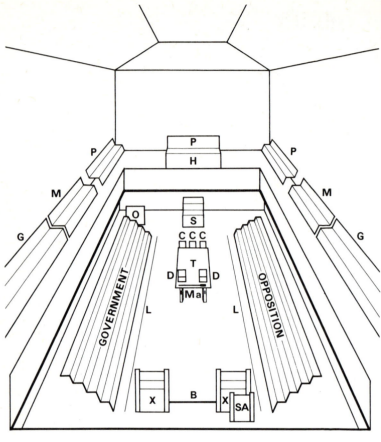

S	Mr. Speaker	**D**	Despatch boxes
P	Press galleries	**Ma**	Mace (when the House goes into Committee, the Mace is put 'below the Table' on hooks)
H	*Hansard* reporters		
O	Government Officials' seats		
C	Clerks of the House (when the House goes into Committee, Mr. Speaker leaves the Chair, and the Chairman sits in the chair of the Clerk of the House, which is the one on the left).	**L**	Lines over which Members may not step when speaking from the front benches
		B	Bar of the House
		X	Cross benches
		SA	Serjeant at Arms
T	Table of the House	**M**	Members' galleries
		G	Visitors' galleries

Fig. 3 The House of Commons

to every citizen at the local public library. Members of the public may sit in the Public Gallery of the Lords or Commons and listen to the debates. In addition there are courses of action which any citizen may take to bring pressure to bear on his elected representative.

7.2 The Opposition

The government, as we have seen, is the party with the largest number of MPs in the Commons. The party with the second largest is the official Opposition. Lesser parties are also in opposition but have no special standing. The Leader of the Opposition is paid a salary in addition to that received as an MP, like a Minister, and has special duties to perform.

It was once said that the nation pays the Prime Minister £14,000 a year to run the country and the Leader of the Opposition £4,500 to prevent him from doing it. The opposition cannot, in fact, prevent the government from governing when, as is usual, the government has a majority of Members to vote its Bills through. It can subject the government to very close scrutiny and criticism and in this it performs a very useful function. The saying that 'it is the duty of the opposition to oppose' should not be taken too literally. Indeed, an opposition that gets a reputation for factious criticism does itself harm. It creates an impression of insincerity, it opens itself to devastating retorts from the government when the latter's case is good, it weakens the impact of its criticism when that criticism is justified. Nevertheless, it must scrutinise and probe, in the interest of good government. The overall policy of the opposition will differ from that of the government. Its most effective work lies in presenting an alternative policy to that of the government and in presenting itself as an alternative administration. Thus when the Chancellor of the Exchequer speaks for the government, the 'shadow' chancellor replies on behalf of the opposition. He may well be a former chancellor. He is the party expert and specialises on questions of national finance. The leader of the opposition (the 'shadow' Prime Minister) tries to ensure that he has experts on every aspect of policy in his team so that his party looks like a possible alternative administration. But despite the surface battle, there is considerable cooperation between the Whips on both sides to ensure the smooth working of Parliament, and there are cross-party friendships among Members. This is not evidence of insincerity or that the disputes are not real: merely that our representatives can respect someone who holds differing views from their own.

7.3 A Bill in Parliament

Parliament is sometimes criticised as 'a talking shop'. 'It is all talk', people say. Actually, the word Parliament comes from the French word 'parler' — to talk. There is certainly a very thorough 'talking out' before a Bill becomes law. But surely, this is a good thing: we should discuss all aspects of a proposal before it becomes binding on us all. Parliamentary talk leads to action, though: it is not 'mere talk'.

Consider the procedure entailed in getting a Bill through Parliament. In 1965 the government of the day — a Labour government — decided that it was necessary to make certain changes in the law relating to trade unions. Because this is such a controversial issue, affecting so many people both in the trade unions and outside, the government decided to set up a Royal Commission to examine the problems and to make recommendations. A Royal Commission is appointed by Royal Warrant and has power to call people and organisations before it to give evidence and be questioned. The Royal Commission on Trade Unions and Employers' Associations was set up in 1965. Its chairman was Lord Donovan, a Lord of Appeal (i.e. a judge, who sits in the House of Lords), and its members included eminent representative employers and trade unionists, university experts on industrial relations, specialists in industrial law, economists, journalists and the headmistress of a comprehensive school to represent the ordinary, thoughtful citizen. The Commission had a staff of civil servants to help it and began by working out a long list of the detailed questions it needed to consider. It took evidence from employers' organisations, trade unions, industrial experts, individual trade unionists and organisations concerned with industrial welfare, and had memoranda submitted to it by an equally wide range of organisations. The Report (Cmd. 3623, HMSO, £1) was published in June 1968. It was a massive volume and contained recommendations on a wide range of topics, including the extension of collective bargaining, strikes (official and unofficial), the safeguard of employees against unfair dismissal, the enforcement of collective agreements, trade union organisation, employers' associations, the establishment of a new organisation, the Industrial Relations Commission to work continuously to promote improvements in relations between employers and employed.

Most of the recommendations were supported by all the members of the Commission but there were some individual reservations on particular points.

Following publication, the Report was discussed in the press, on TV and in countless meetings of trade unionists on the one hand, and employers on the other.

The Secretary of State for Employment and Productivity

IN PLACE OF STRIFE

A POLICY FOR INDUSTRIAL RELATIONS

Presented to Parliament by the First Secretary of State and
Secretary of State for Employment and Productivity
by Command of Her Majesty
January 1969

LONDON
HER MAJESTY'S STATIONERY OFFICE
3s. 6d. net

Cmnd. 3888

Fig. 4 Cover of government White Paper 'In Place of Strife'

(formerly the Minister of Labour) then had to decide which of the recommendations of the Royal Commission she would urge the government to adopt. They were embodied in a draft 'White Paper' which remained confidential while colleagues in the government and organisations especially affected, such as the Trades Union Congress General Council and the Confederation of British Industries, were consulted. Last minute amendments were made in the draft and the White Paper, 'In Place of Strife: A Policy for Industrial Relations' (Cmd. 3888, HMSO, 3s 6d), was issued in January 1969. The debate was renewed in the press. In the better newspapers the White Paper was quoted extensively; in others in summary. Trade union leaders were interviewed and explained why they thought it went too far in interfering in industrial matters: employers' leaders explained why they thought it had not gone far enough — why it was a missed opportunity. (It will be noted that the government cannot expect to please all the parties involved.) Newspaper editors and broadcasting commentators gave their views. Cabinet Ministers brought it into their speeches at the weekends, defending its provisions and announcing it as 'a step forward'.

Some of the proposals in this White Paper, particularly those that sought to impose fines on trade unionists resorting to unconstitutional action, for example, calling wildcat strikes without going through the procedure set out in the union's rules, aroused such deep opposition from the trade unions and many Labour Members of Parliament that they threatened to split the party and were dropped by the government in return for a pledge by the Trades Union Congress to deal themselves with unconstitutional strikes. (Incidentally, the pledge was honoured and unconstitutional strikes fell dramatically.) The less controversial proposals were later embodied in a Bill and brought before Parliament. But before the Bill had been passed into law, the Labour government fell. Its defeat was ascribed, in some quarters, to its 'weakness' in dropping the penal clauses of the Industrial Relations Bill. Its action in doing so is an interesting example of the limitation on government action mentioned in the opening paragraphs of this chapter.

The issue was now with the Conservatives. Their proposals for action in the new Parliament, set out in the Speech delivered by the Queen in opening Parliament on 2 July 1970, included a Bill 'to establish a framework of law within which improved industrial relations can develop' and a code of practice 'laying down standards for good management and trade union practice'.

On 5 October 1970 they issued a Consultative Document detailing their proposals to improve industrial relations and further public discussion followed. The Bill itself was published on 3 December 1970 and formally introduced to the Commons for its First Reading.

The Bill established the individual's right to belong (or not to belong) to a trade union and protection was given against unfair dismissal. Written agreements between unions and employers were to be legally binding unless both sides agreed that they should not be. Trade unions and employers' associations were to register with a government official and unregistered organisations lost some protection for their funds. Registered organisations were to conform to the rules of conduct set down in the code of industrial practice. A National Industrial Relations Court was to be established with powers to award compensation against trade unions or employers which acted illegally. Civil proceedings could be taken in the court against unofficial strike leaders. Legal action would depend on the initiative of individuals, either employers or workers or by unions or employer associations. The government (through the Secretary of State for Employment) was to have reserve powers, to be exercised only in times of emergency, to apply to the National Industrial Relations Court for the declaration of a 'cooling off' period of sixty days to delay industrial action and enable negotiations to proceed, and further, to require a ballot of union members where there was reason to doubt their support for strike action called by their leaders.

The Second Reading of the Bill took place on 14 and 15 December 1970. At this stage the Principles of the Bill, though not its details, were debated. The Minister responsible, Mr Carr, the Secretary of State for Employment and Productivity, said that the Bill was necessary because liberty in some areas had degenerated into licence and a more orderly and disciplined system of industrial relations was required under which freedom would be increased. The opposition claimed that it would do nothing but exacerbate feeling between employers and trade unionists and snarl up industrial relations in a tangle of legal disputes of profit only to lawyers. Further, the legal enforceability of agreements would end the existing informal, flexible system of wage negotiation. The necessity for trade unions to register and the loss of power to make their own rules would end the long period of freedom of association enjoyed by those bodies. The 'closed shop' (under which workers refused to work with non-unionists), now to be prohibited, had helped to provide stable industrial relations. These would be put at risk.

The Second Reading was given on 15 December, the government using its majority to outvote the opposition.

The trade unions organised massed meetings of protest on 12 January 1971 and some unofficial token strikes occurred.

The Bill now proceeded to the Committee Stage in the House of Commons. Most Bills are considered by a Standing Committee — a small group of Members whose numbers are proportional to those of the parties in the House — who meet in a room upstairs and debate the Bill clause by clause. The Industrial Relations Bill, however, being of such importance, was considered by a 'Committee of the Whole House', i.e. all the Members participate and the proceedings take place in the House of Commons but with a chairman and not the usual Speaker in charge. The committee stage started on 18 January 1971. In view of the fact that the opposition had announced its determination to stop the Bill if possible and had put down a great number of detailed amendments to this already long Bill, it was clear that the government would have to take special measures if the Bill was not to be debated indefinitely and time needed for other matters (such as the Budget) and other Bills, used unnecessarily.

There are established procedures to enable a government to limit the amount of time given to such debates. A Minister may move 'the closure' and if he gets a majority of votes (which he does if his party supports him) the debate finishes and a vote is taken. Or he may move 'the Guillotine' which provides for 'closure by compartments', i.e. for taking a vote on parts of a Bill, or on batches of amendments, at a time announced, so that the total time is curtailed but opportunities are given for all parts of the Bill to be discussed though not in the detail the opposition would like. If critics spend too much time on clause 1 then less is available for the other clauses. The Speaker (the protector of minorities in the House) may refuse to accept a 'closure' motion and does so if he thinks it an abuse of the rules of the House, or an infringement of the rights of the minority.

On the Industrial Relations Bill, Mr Whitelaw (Leader of the House, responsible for getting the government's business through) introduced a guillotine motion which gave ten days to the Committee debate and four days to the later Report Stage and Third Reading (see below). The opposition criticised this and moved an amendment that six days be allowed for the later stages and this was accepted by the government. Despite 100 hours of debate on the committee stage, many in the small hours of the morning, 100 of the Bill's 150 clauses were not debated, including those setting up the National Industrial Relations Court and the Commission for Industrial Relations. Naturally, this led to a great deal of criticism from the opposition and the trade unions. The government was accused of trying to 'gag' the opposition and of undemocratic behaviour.

At the Report Stage (that is, when the state of the Bill as it emerged from the Committee was reported to the whole House), which took five days from 15 March to 23 March, the government agreed to introduce many of the suggestions put forward in committee. Accordingly, it added thirteen new clauses to the Bill and tabled ninety amendments. One notable change was that unions of actors and musicians were permitted to operate a 'closed shop', that is, insist on 100 per cent union membership in any cast or orchestra in view of the special difficulties that exist in their field in maintaining trade-union organisation.

The opposition challenged fifty-seven divisions at the end of this stage, that is, it insisted that a vote be taken each time by the usual method of Members 'dividing', i.e. walking into the 'yes' or 'no' lobbies, where their names were recorded and counted. This procedure took hours and was wearisome in the extreme, but is a traditional means of protesting.

The Third Reading, when the principles — as they have emerged from Committee and Report Stages — are debated, took place on 24 March 1971 and the Bill went to the House of Lords.

The experience of the Bill in the Lords illustrates the usefulness of that body: for after a two-day debate on the Second Reading no fewer than eighteen days were given to the committee stage which enabled 340 amendments to be debated out of the 1,100 tabled. Thus the precious time of the Commons was supplemented by that given in the Lords and the Bill emerged in a much better condition in consequence. The Bill was given an unopposed Third Reading in the Lords and then went back to the Commons.

The changes made in the Lords then had to be considered at a second Report Stage in the Commons. This took five days between 28 July and 4 August. Discussion proceeded under a guillotine motion which stopped debate at midnight each evening and ended discussion with a single vote on 4 August. Of the 340 amendments accepted in the Lords and now considered in the Commons, 135 were new government proposals or proposals accepted by the government from the opposition, thirty-two improved the wording and 137 were necessary as a consequence of changes previously made.

The Bill having received the approval of both Houses of Parliament, it was submitted for formal approval by the Queen. The Royal Assent was given on 5 August 1971 and the Bill thus became law.

This brief account of the passage of the Industrial Relations Bill illustrates the process by which an idea, or set of ideas, becomes a policy and, after intense discussion both in and out of Parliament, eventually becomes law. A mere recital of all the stages through which a Bill has to pass gives the impression that Parliament is tied up in out-dated and useless procedures: but when an actual Bill is considered the necessity of each stage is more apparent.

It is important that a Bill which may affect our freedom — for example, as trade unionists or as employers — should be scrutinised closely. Of course, the government of the day usually gets its way: but not before its actions are exposed for all to see and usually not before it has accepted many of the opposition's criticisms. And the opposition, if it is still not satisfied, can declare its intention to repeal the Bill when it next comes into office.

7.4 Question Time

One of the most important means of keeping the government on its
toes is 'Question Time'. On every day except Friday, the afternoon
session in the Commons opens with questions. Any Member of Parliament may submit, in writing, a question to a Minister. The answers are
prepared by civil servants but the Minister must be well briefed beyond
the narrow point of the question because the questioner first, and then
any other MP has the right to ask 'supplementary' questions. A
Minister's reputation may be enhanced (or diminished) by the manner
in which he stands up to 'supplementaries'.

Some questions are designed simply to get at the facts, as when a
Member asks the Secretary of State for Education and Science how
many children are taking school meals, or when he proposes to raise the
school-leaving age. Or it may be to urge a particular course of action.
Thus, on 23 July 1970, Mr Cronin asked the Secretary of State for
Education and Science if she would take steps to phase out corporal
punishment in schools.

Mr van Straubenzee, the Under Secretary, replying on behalf of
Mrs Thatcher, the Secretary of State, said: 'In my view this is properly
within the discretion of local authorities and teachers.'

Mr Cronin, not satisfied with this reply, came back with a supplementary question: 'Is the Under Secretary aware,' he asked, 'that in
almost no other European country is corporal punishment permitted?
Is not corporal punishment in schools unnecessary, does it not teach
children to approve of physical violence and does it not often lead to
sadistic practices?'

Mr van Straubenzee was unmoved by these arguments: 'I am well
aware,' he said, 'that this is a matter which arouses strong feelings on
both sides, but I still think it is better left in the way I first suggested.'
Mr Cronin was so dissatisfied that he gave notice that he would bring
the matter up again in the debate on the adjournment at the end of the
day, when Members have the opportunity to initiate discussion on
topics of concern.

Some questions are not designed to elicit information but to give
the questioner the opportunity to make a general attack on the government in a supplementary question. Thus, Mrs Renee Short, on 16 July
1970, soon after the new Conservative government had taken office,
asked the Secretary of State for Employment and Productivity if he
would bring forward the date for the full implementation of equal pay
for women.

Mr Robert Carr, the Minister concerned, probably sensing that
there was something behind this question, answered shortly. 'No.
Madam.' Mrs Short then put in the knife: 'In view of the Prime

Minister's [Mr Heath's] recently discovered interest in women and housewives,' she said, 'and as many women voted him into office, does not the Rt. Hon. Gentleman think that he ought to change his views about this matter and give women a fair reward for the job they do in industry and bring forward the date for the implementation of equal pay?'

Mr Carr remained unmoved: 'This was one of the matters on which I agreed with the Rt. Hon. Lady, my predecessor [Mrs Barbara Castle],' he said. 'I think that the five-year period which was set in the Equal Pay Act is about right.'

Questions are a means of bringing pressure on the government to tackle urgent problems. Thus, Mr Frank Allaun asked the Minister of Public Buildings and Works how many building trade operatives were out of work and what steps he was taking to provide them with work. Mr Heffer had a similar question down for answering. Mr Julian Amery, the Minister, replied that there were 93,718 persons unemployed in the construction industry in June 1970. Their prospects were bound up with those of the economy as a whole. Meanwhile the Ministry of Housing was seeking to stimulate demand for house improvement through local authorities.

Mr Allaun retorted that this was not good enough. The Minister should press his colleagues to take the brakes off house building, both private and council, so that the unemployed and ill-housed could both benefit.

Mr Amery said that he would do his best and commented that when the Conservatives were in office in 1964 unemployment in the building trade was less than half that existing when they took over from Labour in 1970.

Mr Heffer pressed for a four-fold course of action: would the Minister discuss the whole matter with the builders as the Labour Minister had done? Would he press for the abolition of the Selective Employment Tax? Would he give maximum assistance to council house building? Would he give financial assistance to the small builder?

Mr Amery said he had already consulted both sides of the industry and thanked Mr Heffer for support on the abolition of SET (a matter in which Mr Heffer was going against the policy of his own party).

Questions on the Order Paper (which sets out the business for the day) not answered orally when the time allotted for them has expired are answered in writing. The more supplementaries are asked, the fewer questions will be dealt with orally. Hence tripping questions which get nowhere and unhelpful supplementaries are unpopular with Members seeking oral answers.

A glance at *Hansard* will indicate the wide spread of questions asked in any one day: from matters concerning one ordinary citizen to our relations with foreign powers, from unemployment in Dorset to strikes in the motor industry, from the closure of a local hospital to the provision of more publicity for the cervical smear test, for protection of the public from promoters of package tour holidays to the spread of violence at football matches, from the state of the lavatories in a primary school in Boston Spa to the escape of a prisoner from Brixton gaol.

The government has to answer for its actions, explain its proposals and generally show that it is conducting the affairs of the nation fairly and effectively.

7.5 Parliamentary procedure

There are many proposals for making the work of Parliament more efficient. People have questioned the wisdom of all-night sittings. Morning sittings were introduced, but not universally welcomed, especially by Members who continued their former occupations, and were later discontinued. This raises the question as to whether Members of Parliament should regard membership as a full-time job. Many Members cannot continue their old jobs — miners, for example. But the need for the House of Commons to be a reflection of the nation with Members from all parts of the country, all classes and all occupations supports the case of those who wish to keep in touch with their former work. Whether they can do both jobs properly is another question.

Another suggestion is that further specialist committees should be set up to deal with matters that do not receive sufficient time in the House: it is suggested that they would enable back-bench Members to get more information from Ministers and have a greater influence on policymaking than they now have. The establishment of extra committees that had to meet when the House was sitting led to complaints that Members were unable to be in the Commons at important times and that the work of the committees was frequently interrupted as Members dashed away to vote on the matters being considered in the Commons.

Suggestions have also been made that the voting procedure could be speeded up by the use of electronic devices. This also has its difficulties because Members are frequently some way from the voting lobbies when a vote takes place, and time would still need to be given to enable them to reach the place where the button had to be pushed. However, it would save them tramping in and out of the voting lobbies for hour after hour as sometimes happens at present.

Questions *for discussion and action*

1. Watch the Parliamentary reports in one of the better papers. When a topic that interests you arises (for example, a Bill regulating the tattooing of teenagers, or censorship, or industrial relations, or changes in taxation, or the control of immigration, or race-relations) get a copy of *Hansard* for that day and read the debate in full. Better still, attend a debate on the subject in the House of Commons or the House of Lords. This can be done by writing to your MP for a ticket, or going down to the House and queuing.

    Now consider the statement (p. 51) that 'the government has to justify its acts before a highly critical audience [meaning the Members] in the House of Commons and the Lords'.

2. Obtain from Her Majesty's Stationery Office a White Paper explaining any Bill that the government is about to introduce, or reporting action taken. Summarise it; give a talk to your group at college or work, indicating your approval or disapproval of the action proposed or taken.

    NB. A visit to any of Her Majesty's Stationery Offices is well worthwhile. Publications range from ordnance survey maps to reproductions of paintings in the national art collections, scientific and economic publications, career guides, information on Commonwealth countries, United Nations publications, descriptions of borstals and approved schools in addition to the regular daily and weekly *Hansard*s.

3. Examine *Hansard* for a recent date and note the questions put and answers given, both oral and written. Estimate their value. Classify the questioners in accordance with your own scale of values; for example:

G.S.A.T.	(Genuine seeker after truth)
I.C.	(Indefatigable campaigner)
L.S.G.	(Loyal supporter of the government)
T.T.	(Tricky tripper)
F.W.	(Fatuous windbag).

    (To avoid actions for slander these should be kept to yourself.)

4. Consider the functions of the Opposition. Give examples of successful pressure by the Opposition:
    (a) To secure the withdrawal of some proposed government action;
    (b) To secure fresh action by the government;
    (c) To bring down a government.

Chapter 8

The Member of Parliament and his constituents

8.1 An MP not a mere mouthpiece

A Member of Parliament is not a mere mouthpiece for the people who have elected him, whose job is to find out what his constituents wish on every issue and vote accordingly. If this was all that was required it would be better to employ a computer. No. An MP should have a mind of his own and use it. He is elected to Parliament to support the policies and principles of his party. He must be left to judge just how and when they can be implemented in the changing circumstances of our political and economic life.

That a Member is not a delegate with detailed instructions from his constituents, but a representative with his own mind and judgement was a doctrine put (in the rather flowery language of the day) by Edmund Burke in a speech [1] to the electors of Bristol, on being declared a Member for that city on 3 November 1774:

Certainly, gentlemen, it ought to be the happiness and glory of a representative to live in the strictest union, the closest correspondence, and the most unreserved communication with his constituents. Their wishes ought to have great weight with him; their opinion, high respect; their business, unremitted attention. It is his duty to sacrifice his repose, his pleasures, his satisfaction, to theirs; and above all, ever, and in all cases to prefer their interest to his own. But his unbiased opinion, his mature judgement, his enlightened conscience, he ought not to sacrifice to you, to any man, or to any set of men living. These he does not derive from your pleasure; no, nor from the law and the constitution. They are a trust from providence, for the abuse of which he is deeply answerable. Your representative thus owes you, not his industry only, but his judgement; and he betrays, instead of serving you, if he sacrifices it to your opinion.

8.2 An MP and the views of his constituents

Having said all this, it must also be clear that a Member, if he wishes to remain a Member, may not flout the opinion of his constituents on non-political issues such as divorce, homosexuality, the death penalty, to such an extent that they will not vote for him again. He will, of course, seek to further the interests of his constituency. If he is in a town where cars are manufactured he will be found speaking up when the interests of the car industry are discussed. He will be approached by the association of motor-car manufacturers and given facts in support of their claims. The trade unions affected will also ask his support. But his decision should be on what is best for the country as a whole.

Many organised groups of people will put their case to him and seek his aid: the churches, the licensed victuallers, old age pensioners, organisations for the improvement of state education, teachers, youth organisations, opponents of blood sports, the Campaign for Nuclear Disarmament, the Campaign against Racial Discrimination, the local branch of the United Nations Association, the Prison Visitors Association and so on. Naturally, the Member will be concerned, not only with

Member of Parliament being consulted by his constituents

the issues raised by these organisations, but by the weight of opinion behind them. The churches are still powerful in this country. The Roman Catholic Church, in particular, is very much concerned to maintain its own schools where its particular beliefs can be taught. In a constituency with a large Roman Catholic community a Member will be anxious not to antagonise this large and highly organised section of his supporters: they are thus able to 'put pressure' on him. Sometimes, of course, he resists that pressure. Baroness (Dr) Summerskill recalls [2] that in the general election of 1935, when she stood at Bury, in Lancashire, for Labour, four Roman Catholic priests offered the support of their flock, many of them Labour-inclined, on condition that she promised not, in future, to teach birth-control to any woman. This she rejected, indignantly. The next Sunday they preached in favour of the Conservative candidate. She commented that the Conservative and Liberal candidates, with families of two children respectively, satisfied the priests that they had no sympathy with family planning. 'It would seem,' she concluded, 'that in their case a beneficent providence achieves the same results as "birth control" does in mine.' Of course, in a constituency with a large Roman Catholic electorate the parties are likely to have a large Catholic membership and probably Catholic candidates, when such pressures become unnecessary.

Examples of the effectiveness of collective action in 'bringing pressure to bear' abound, from the efforts of a town to secure a new steel works or prevent the closing of its major industry, to the classic case of the Stansted agitation, where local groups and their MPs stopped the siting of a massive third London airport in a rural Essex area — and this after the Minister had repeatedly refused to budge.

8.3 An MP and his local political party

Among the most effective of the pressure groups are the political parties. A Member depends on the slogging work of his local party members to keep the organisation in good trim and to conduct his election campaign with enthusiasm. These 'activists' are usually very politically conscious, with decided and often extreme party views. Their opinions will naturally weigh heavily with the Member. Keen supporters of a political policy should, therefore, get into their local parties if they wish to influence policy and particularly the policy of their Member. Much is heard of party discipline at Westminster and the pressure brought by party Whips to secure conformity to the party line; that is, the official policy of the party. A Member must weigh up the importance of the issue, and if his party is in office consider whether or not his vote may result in the defeat of the government before voting against the majority of his party.

From time to time rebels do emerge and sometimes vote in defiance of the Whips. It is surprising how often one notes that the following weekend they have met their local party executive and received their support. This does not always happen. In Lincoln in 1972 the local Labour Party took issue with their Member of Parliament, Dick Taverne, over his support for Britain's entry into the European Economic Community in defiance of the Labour Party's collective decision against it. He was one of some fifty Labour Members who supported it and were prepared to vote against the decision of the Parliamentary Labour Party on grounds similar to those quoted from Edmund Burke at the beginning of this chapter: that their minds and consciences were, in matters of high principle, to be put above party decisions. Mr Taverne decided to resign his seat and fight a by-election to determine whether or not he had the support of the electors. He was disowned by the local Labour Party, who put up a candidate against him, but he secured an overwhelming majority in the by-election of February 1973. It is interesting to note that most of the other dissentiants on this issue did not come into violent conflict with their local parties.

Parties are probably more open to the pressure of rank-and-file opinion and internal pressures shortly after the party has been defeated at a general election. The party sits back to think out why it lost. What old policies must be jettisoned? What new policies are required? The fundamentalists in the party will bring out the pure milk of traditional doctrine. New thinkers will battle for the adoption of new ideas. Out of this ferment will come a new orthodoxy.

The victorious party, especially if it was wise enough not to make too many promises at the election, comes in with the opportunity to try new policies. Advice will be showered on it by organised business, by the trade unions, by consumer organisations, teachers, taxpayers, investors, borrowers, who hope that, with a fresh start, the new government will lean their way.

8.4 The citizen and his MP

While group action is generally more effective than individual, an individual elector should not hesitate to approach his MP if he has anything important to say. Most MPs are punctilious in replying to correspondence and will often seize the occasion to state at length their views or their party's views on the issue raised. An elector may also 'lobby' his Member, that is, go into the Member's Lobby in the House of

Commons, send in a 'green card' to his Member and thus call him out to discuss his complaint. 'Mass Lobbying' is the same operation carried out by an organised group who may sometimes be seen buzzing around their Members in the Lobby like angry wasps. The fact that not many unattached people (that is, not members of political parties or of organised groups like CND) write or call to see their MPs on matters of policy, as distinct from personal problems, adds weight to the actions of those who do. A letter beginning, 'I have never written to an MP before, but feel I must protest against . . .' is bound to be read with respect. In times of exceptional concern, such as the abdication of King Edward VIII in 1936, MPs receive a large volume of correspondence, which helps them judge public feeling. Most MPs keep a keen eye on their local paper. A letter to the editor that stirs up a correspondence is an effective way of getting his support.

Some MPs make an attempt to keep in contact with local opinion by holding regular public meetings to 'report back' to their constituents on Parliamentary affairs, hoping to get some indication of public reaction to events. However, the greater part of the audience is usually made up of party activists: the ordinary, not-particularly political citizen rarely turns out between elections. But if he does not bother, he can hardly grumble if his opinion is not considered.

Questions *for discussion and action*

1. Examine the local paper and make a list of the organisations mentioned there that have as one of their purposes the influencing of Members of Parliament. Note the objects they are promoting.

2. Examine the 'Letters to the Editor'. Which do you think are persuasive? Which unconvincing?

3. Discuss any local issue (such as a lack of facilities for sport, swimming, social life) and write a letter to the local newspaper, councillor or your MP urging action.

4. Study the national press: collect examples of 'pressure' on the government to achieve certain purposes: e.g. changes in taxation, the building of more roads; improvements in education; the prohibition of advertisements for cigarettes.

5. Make a study in depth of any successful agitation such as the Stansted operation, which achieved its purpose.

6. Analyse the correspondence in *The Times*. List the 'causes' that are being advocated. Note the status of the correspondents. Do you think that a letter to *The Times* would have more weight than a letter in one of the popular papers? If so, why?

7. Examine the letters column in the *Daily Mirror*. Consider the

statement: 'A letter to *The Times* is addressed to the government: in the popular press to the other readers.'

8. Inquire at the local public library and make a directory of local organisations catering for your age group, noting the youth sections of the political parties as well as youth, cultural and sports clubs.

9. Consider the establishment of a 'New Voters' Group' for people getting the vote for the first time at the next general election, with a view to the discussion of basic political issues: invite speakers from the main political parties.

10. If you are in an organised group (such as a sixth form or class in a college of further education, or a youth organisation) invite your local MP to speak to you on, 'How the ordinary citizen can make his wishes felt'.

Chapter 9

The redress of grievances

9.1 Writing to your MP

The previous chapter shows how an individual citizen may bring pressure to bear on his Member of Parliament to ensure that his — the citizen's — views are taken into account when new laws are being considered or when specific acts of government (such as the determination of pension or tax rates) are being decided.

The individual citizen may also ask his Member of Parliament to check on government departments with whom the citizen has had unsatisfactory dealings. For example, his daughter may wish to become a teacher but has been unable to get into a college of education: she has the necessary A levels — there seems to be some bias against her. Will the Member please investigate? Or perhaps he has not been able to get a rent allowance from the local council under the Housing Finance Act, though he is clearly entitled to one. Will the Member see why they are dragging their feet? Or perhaps a deserted wife and mother has had her Social Security stopped. Will the Member please look into it?

Most Members of Parliament attend regularly at Advice Centres, sometimes referred to as 'Surgeries', in their constituencies where citizens may consult them on such problems. Some inquirers, for example those wanting advice on personal or domestic matters, are referred to specialised organisations such as the Family Welfare Association or the Citizen's Advice Bureau: but the conscientious Member of Parliament has a considerable number of inquiries always on his desk: as he clears one, further inquiries come in and the variety of subjects on which he is asked for help grows.

There are other means by which grievances may be redressed: the most important is the Law; others are through the numerous tribunals set up to consider grievances that arise from the acts of officials who have to carry out in detail policies set out broadly in various acts of Parliament, many concerned with the social services. There are also the consultative bodies through which pressure can be brought on the nationalised industries; and when all else fails, there is the Parliamentary Commissioner or Ombudsman, a 'long stop' for inquiring into grievances that arise from maladministration in government departments.

9.2 The Law

As we saw in Chapter 1, there are two branches of law: the criminal and the civil. The criminal law is concerned with behaviour, such as stealing or murder, which, though committed against an individual, is regarded as harmful to society as a whole and action is taken against the wrongdoer in the name of society. The civil law is concerned with disputes between individuals and action here is taken by the aggrieved party.

It is through the civil courts, then, that the individual citizen is likely to turn to redress a grievance he may have against a trader for goods not up to standard, for compensation for damage, in matrimonial and similar disputes. Accordingly, his first contact with 'the law' may well be in the local county court. Every citizen should familiarise himself with the workings of these courts. There are about 400 of them throughout the country and one can pop in for half an hour at any time when they are in session.

The courts are presided over by about 100 county court judges. The judge, wigged and gowned and wearing a purple sash, sits on an elevated bench at the front of the court facing the public. He is referred to as 'His Honour' and addressed as 'Your Honour'. Below him is his clerk. There are places to the left for the parties to the disputes. Facing the judge are rows of seats (like pews in a non-conformist chapel): in the front rows are barristers in gowns and wigs and solicitors in gowns only. The public sits behind.

Perhaps the first case is one arising from a 'judgment summons' obtained by a local radio firm against a customer who is behind with his HP payments and refuses to pay the amount judged by the court on a previous occasion to be due. The young man says he is unemployed; he is married with three children; his pay is not high. The judge patiently probes for the facts, gets at the overtime and bonus earned as well as basic pay; notes the amount of family allowance; establishes that the man is not now unemployed and was unemployed for two weeks only.

The payments are in respect of a TV set, two transistor radios and a record player. The judge suggests that he has done himself rather well and turns a critical eye on the shopkeeper. He orders payment of the regular instalments plus 50p a week off the arrears.

The next case concerns a collision between two lorries, the purpose being to apportion blame so that 'damages' may be apportioned similarly. Here barristers are at work questioning, cross-questioning, re-examining the witnesses, where needed, in an effort to get at the truth. In this case the pertinent witnesses are the lorry drivers and their mates. Finally, counsel have asked their last questions and summed up their cases. The judge apportions blame as to 60 per cent and 40 per cent and the lorry drivers go outside, exchange cigarettes and natter over the case before going back to work.

A third case may be for the possession of a room let by a householder to a 'foreign lady'. At first the judge's sympathies are clearly with the tenant — he suspects prejudice against her — but her admission to pouring water over the landlady's baby and general revelation of mental instability lead to an order for possession with the probation officer asked to see what can be done for the poor disturbed woman.

A morning in the court will impress most observers with the unhurried care with which each case is considered: the scrupulous search for the facts and the desire to see fair play.

Appeal can be made against the decision of the county court to the appeal court. More serious cases are taken in the first instance to the High Court of Justice, from which there is also right of appeal to the superior court and the House of Lords. The system of civil courts may be depicted thus:

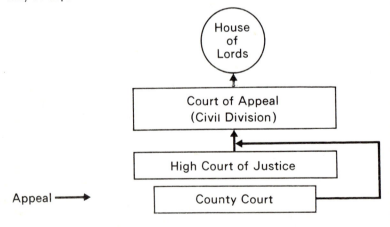

Fig. 5 The Civil Courts

One may, of course, seek protection through the criminal law. A woman has been beaten by her husband and goes to the police for protection. Here the police bring the charge (in the name of the Queen). The husband would be summoned to the local magistrates' court (formerly known as the police court). Here, as the name implies, magistrates preside. Magistrates, or justices of the peace, are local people, often nominated by the political parties, chosen for their judgement and experience, whose names have been put forward by a local advisory committee to the Lord Chancellor, with whom the appointment lies. They are people with a wide and varied experience of life but with no professional legal training. In recent years they have been expected to attend courses to equip themselves for their exacting — and, it should be noted, unpaid — work.

In some areas, notably in London and other large cities, it is not possible to find enough suitable people with time for this work. Here, there are Stipendiary (or full-time, paid) magistrates, all barristers of at least seven years' experience.

The magistrates, whether lay or stipendiary, sit on a raised 'bench' at the front of the court. There are usually three 'lay' magistrates, though the stipendiary magistrate may sit alone. Below the magistrates is the clerk, who advises on legal points. Naturally the lay magistrates depend very much on him, though the responsibility for all decisions is theirs.

A visit to the local magistrates' court is well worth while. The first cases before the court are the drunks picked up by the police the previous evening. The formalities are quickly over: one by one they plead guilty, are fined, ask for time to pay and shuffle off with the policeman or policewoman according to sex.

Then comes a more extended case. Two lads of eighteen and nineteen are accused of stealing a car and, on being chased by the police, of crashing it into a lamp-post. Evidence is given by the police, the boys admit their guilt. The magistrate asks the boys if they can pay for the damage done. They have no savings. Did they think what anxiety they have caused the owner? Did they realise what danger they caused to innocent passers by? The lads cannot reply. The probation officer speaks up for them. They have not been in trouble before. The elder wants to join the Army and will probably be accepted. The younger was led away by the elder. The magistrate defers sentence for two weeks: if the elder gets into the Army that will be that: the younger is put on probation.

Next comes the case where the wife has been assaulted by her husband. This is a serious charge and the court has to decide if there is a case to answer: if so, the accused will be 'committed' to a higher court for trial. Both sides are represented by counsel, the police by a trim young woman barrister and the accused by a solicitor. Evidence is given of the complaint being made, the approach by the police to the husband who is alleged to have seized a flat-iron and hit one of the policemen with it. (The policeman's head is still in bandages.) Evidence is corroborated, written down and confirmed. The solicitor for the husband suggests that the police assaulted his client and that there is no case to answer. The magistrates consult together, ask advice of the clerk to the court and announce that they 'commit the accused for trial at the crown court'.

Crown courts (formerly called assizes or quarter sessions) are higher courts where more serious cases are dealt with. Here, a judge presides (sometimes assisted by local magistrates), there is more formality, the barristers appearing in wigs and gowns; questions of fact are decided by juries but the judges pronounce on questions of law and decide the sentences. Appeals go to the Court of Appeal, and, if necessary, the House of Lords.

The system of Criminal Courts may be illustrated thus:

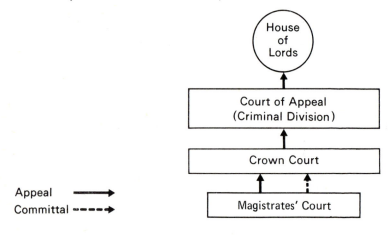

Fig. 6 The Criminal Courts

A new court, established under the Industrial Relations Act 1971, which will sit in all parts of the country as required, may well prove to be widely used for the redress of grievances. It has the status of a High Court and it is probable that cases brought before it will be initiated by trade unions or employers rather than individuals who will go in the first instance to Industrial Relations Tribunals (see next section) on more personal matters such as wrongful dismissal.

Many people are reluctant to take a matter to law: they fear they may be involved in heavy costs and end up worse off than before. They fear that tricky lawyers on the other side will make them look foolish. In point of fact, 'Legal Aid' for people of limited means has been available since 1949. Its extent has been increased over the years so that now it is relatively easy to obtain aid to fight a civil case or defend a criminal charge. However, it was not until the Legal Advice and Assistance Act of 1972 that the services of a solicitor were similarly obtainable for work not necessarily involving litigation; for example, in preparing a will or writing letters or giving advice. Assistance may be obtained free by people on Supplementary Benefit (under National Assistance) or receiving the Family Income Supplement. Above that level a charge may be made according to income (and savings) and family responsibility.

A solicitor giving advice under the Act usually displays a sign thus:

Fig. 7 Sign indicating where Legal Advice may be obtained

and it is an invitation to the person requiring advice to walk in and make inquiries. Anyone in doubt should go to the local Citizen's Advice Bureau (address obtainable in the public library or local post office) who will make a preliminary investigation of the case and refer him to a solicitor operating the service. Some local councils have set up legal advice centres, usually in working-class areas, which are manned by full-time lawyers who specialise in the sort of Rent Act queries and maintenance and hire-purchase problems that worry ordinary people but which are often let go by default. The offices are open in the evenings and at shopping hours over the weekend so that they may be visited without loss of working time. The atmosphere is informal and friendly. If the present experiments are successful centres may well be established generally throughout the country and do something to counter the feeling among some people that the law is not for them.

A word is necessary here about the police, the body responsible for the maintenance of 'law and order', whose duty it is to catch people who break the law and bring them before the courts. Again, in some areas, there is the feeling that they are 'against us'. Many youths think that the police 'have it in for them'. They are moved on unnecessarily when chatting at the street corner. They feel that the police always look at them suspiciously. They believe that if they are picked up and taken to the police station there is a fair chance that they will be beaten up.

Of course, some people engage in mildly 'criminal' activities. They 'knock-off' things at work; they are prepared to buy cheap lines that are fairly certainly stolen; they take a chance in not paying a bus or railway fare. Some people do this systematically. They must expect the law to be after them.

The police in many areas seek to establish friendly public relations, especially with young people. They are usually very willing to talk to groups in clubs or colleges of further education about their job and in doing so dispel many myths about themselves. In some areas they help with local sports activities and 'youth adventure' schemes. There is still much suspicion of them in 'coloured' areas and among hippie squatters who are suspected of drug offences. This is probably inevitable so long as there are people who do not feel themselves to be full members of our society.

9.3 Administrative tribunals

Many Acts of Parliament give authority to the Minister concerned to make orders and regulations on matters that are too detailed or too technical to be included in the Act. Others empower local authorities, railway boards and other public bodies to make by-laws. These regulations and by-laws have the force of law and if one breaks them and, for example, damages railway property or a telephone kiosk, or travels without a ticket one may be taken to court.

But many of the regulations are concerned with the social services and the Acts of Parliament that authorised the regulations also set up Administrative Tribunals to which an aggrieved person may appeal and secure speedy redress. There is, for example, the National Insurance Tribunal. A person believing that the local insurance officer has not given him the benefit to which he is entitled may appeal to the National Insurance Tribunal. As the word suggests (tri - bunal), this is a 'court' of three persons: a chairman, who is a lawyer, and two others, one representing employers and the other employees. The procedure at these 'courts' is informal, applicants are put at their ease, and the costs are at a minimum since lawyers are not required. If the decision of the Tribunal is disputed, appeal may be made to the National Insurance Commissioner and sometimes to the Minister. Appeals may also be made to this tribunal in respect of claims for industrial injuries.

Under the Rent Act 1965 a tenant or landlord may apply to the rent officer (usually at the Town Hall) to fix a 'fair rent'. If one party thinks the assessment unfair he may appeal to a Rent Tribunal or Rent Assessment Committee. The members are a chairman (a lawyer) and one surveyor or valuer and one lay person. It is advisable to be represented by a lawyer before this body because the arguments put forward are often highly technical.

Redundancy payments may now be claimed, under an Act of Parliament passed in 1965, by an employee who has been dismissed or kept on short time because his job has become redundant. If he disputes the amount offered he may appeal to a Redundancy Tribunal. These sit in centres all over the country and have a legal chairman and one representative of workers and one of employers. It is usual to have a lawyer or trade union official to put one's case.

The Industrial Relations Act 1971 provides for tribunals to consider such matters as an individual's complaint concerning trade union membership or unfair dismissal by an employer and it has been anticipated that many thousands of appeals will be heard each year.

When the Legal Advice and Assistance Act 1972 came into force in April 1973 there was widespread criticism that it failed to help people who needed legal representation before some of the tribunals mentioned in this section — a serious gap in the legal aid scheme since the tribunals are not uniformly helpful to the persons appearing before them, though legal aid would be available for appeals from the tribunal to the Industrial Relations Court.

9.4 Consumer councils

In addition to the tribunals described in the previous section, there are committees set up under various acts of Parliament to protect the interests of the 'consumers' of products, or services provided by some of the nationalised industries. Thus, there are two coal consumer's councils, one for industrial users of coal and the other for domestic users, which act as a channel for complaints and recommendations to the Coal Board.

There are area consultative councils for the gas and electricity industries through which complaints can be made: and the gas and electricity corporations consult them about proposed changes.

British Rail and London Transport have similar 'users' councils: some people think them useless — so much eyewash. However, they hold public inquiries about such matters as the closure of stations or lines and it is impressive to visit them. Perhaps London Transport has suggested closing a station on the grounds that its use is so slight that its cost is not warranted. The local council will have briefed a lawyer on behalf of local citizens. The statistics put forward by the board are challenged. A large local company has employed a lawyer to put the case for their staff: and how will they be able to recruit staff if there is no near transport? A technical college shows that its students, who come from all over London for specialist studies, will have to walk an extra half-mile each way if the station is closed. One woman – an enterprising local citizen – asks how the members of the committee would like to walk the dark and lonely streets from the next station on a wintry Saturday night after an evening in the West End. The committee recommends that the station should remain open for a further six months. The outcome is that the station is kept open by the board on weekdays although closed on Sundays.

9.5 Tribunals of inquiry

Public tragedies, such as the Aberfan disaster of 1966 when 144 children and adults were engulfed by a moving mountain of sludge, or the events of Bloody Sunday in Londonderry in 1972 when thirteen people were shot dead led to a demand for inquiry so that the facts could be established beyond doubt and action taken where negligence or irregularity was revealed. Pressure is usually stimulated by the press and Members of Parliament take up the case and press the government to set up a tribunal of inquiry under the Tribunals of Inquiry Act 1921. These are usually presided over by a high court judge and have power to call witnesses and for the production of documents.

The reports issued do not always satisfy the public (for example, the Widgery Tribunal on the events in Londonderry was accused in some quarters of whitewashing the Army) but they make it very difficult for any major act of negligence to be covered up.

9.6 The Parliamentary Commissioner or Ombudsman

What redress have we against the action of a civil servant acting in a high-handed or even illegal manner? Well, first we can ask our MP to take the matter up with the government department concerned. If he is unable to get satisfaction and still feels that an injustice has been done, he can refer the case to the Parliamentary Commissioner, or Ombudsman. This official can probe very much more deeply into the work of government departments than a Member of Parliament. He is appointed by the government but is independent of it. He has powers to call a civil servant or Minister before him and ask for information and may cross-examine him, very much as in a court of law. He makes a report to the Member of Parliament who has asked him to take up the case and makes recommendations. In special cases he can make a report direct to Parliament. He issues a report on his work annually.

It is interesting to note how we came to have an Ombudsman in this country. Some land belonging to a farmer at Crichel Down, in Dorset, was compulsorily purchased by the Ministry of Agriculture in 1937 and used during the Second World War and after as a bombing range. The farmer tried to buy back the land for his own use in 1952. He met with difficulties and obstruction but by persistent pressure through his Member of Parliament secured the setting up of a Parliamentary Inquiry into his complaint. The report that followed criticised certain civil servants and the Minister of Agriculture, as the responsible Minister, resigned. In 1961 'Justice', an organisation of lawyers which seeks to improve the operation of the law, investigated the office of Ombudsman in Sweden and other countries. This official has the special duty of inquiring into complaints of maladministration in the public service. They recommended the appointment of a similar official here and the Parliamentary Commissioner Act of 1967 adopted the suggestion.

Complaints are not made directly to the Ombudsman by the aggrieved citizen but to his Member of Parliament. It was thought that direct appeal might weaken the link between the citizen and his Member and that it was important to maintain this link. The Member then decides whether or not to submit the case to the Ombudsman.

No cases of scandalous maladministration have been disclosed since the Ombudsman was appointed, which is a general tribute to the Civil Service, but many cases which otherwise would have festered in some citizen's mind have been cleared up. The annual reports of the Ombudsman show that the largest number of complaints are against the Inland Revenue, the department responsible for assessing income and other taxes. The 1972 report showed that in that year nineteen administrative practices affecting ten government departments were changed to the benefit of the public, partly or wholly due to the Ombudsman's intervention.

In concluding, it is worth noting that the refusal of the farmer at Crichel Down to 'take' what he thought was an injustice, has led, not only to the redress of his own grievance, but to the redress of many other people's. And perhaps even more important to an underlining of the fact that civil servants are indeed the servants of the public and not a law unto themselves.

Questions *for discussion and action*

1. Watch the local paper for notices of any public inquiries to be held in your locality; for example, on proposals to close a railway station or local railway line, to build a motorway through the area, to purchase land, houses or flats compulsorily for council development, to close or divert a footpath.

   Attend as an interested member of the public.

   See if a report appears in your local paper.

2. Visit the local magistrates', county or crown courts. (If a group is involved it is better to write to the clerk or usher beforehand: arrangements can then be made to ensure that the party has seats, or attends a court where the cases are interesting, or at an interesting stage. Some cases are extremely boring.)

   Following the visit, discuss:

   (a) The advantages and disadvantages of having 'lay' magistrates;

   (b) Whether or not legal representation is an advantage. If an advantage, should it be free to all?

   (c) Whether the jury system leads to too many people being acquitted.

   Invite a lay magistrate, a juvenile court magistrate and a probation officer to talk to the group.

3. Discuss in your group their experience of the local police. If dissatisfaction is expressed, arrange for a local police officer to attend and talk about his work and bring up questions (thought out beforehand).

Chapter 10

The systems of government in some other countries

In the course of our history we have had many forms of government — from absolute monarchy, when the king governed by 'divine right', to limited monarchy, when the king was subject to constraint by Parliament; dictatorship, under Cromwell; aristocracy, when Parliament was effectively controlled by the aristocratic landed families — and now democracy, or 'rule by the people'.

Are we to assume that we have now come to the end of the line and that we can expect our form of democracy to go on for ever? We should be well advised not to take it for granted. The Greek philosopher Plato noted how easily the democracies of his day gave way to tyranny. We have seen many countries in Africa and elsewhere start with democratic institutions and rapidly come under the rule of military dictators. It will be useful if we look at a few countries other than our own and see if we can learn anything from their experiences.

10.1 The United States of America

The Constitution of the United States differs from ours in two important respects: it is written; ours is unwritten; it provides for the 'separation of powers' (see below), whereas ours has a greater concentration of powers. New countries like to set down in writing the form of government they propose to establish: it helps them to know where they are. In this country the system of government has evolved. There are many documents dealing with particular issues: Magna Carta, the Bill of

Rights, the Reform Acts (dealing with the right to vote), the Statute of Westminster 1931 (formalising our relations with the self-governing dominions); nevertheless most of the rules are unwritten and based on precedent or what has happened before. It has grown up to meet situations as they occur. When a new situation arises we can depart from precedent and meet it in a new way: we are not tied down to unsuitable courses of action merely because they are written into a constitution. We can act swiftly in a crisis without going through the long procedures laid down for the amendment of a written constitution. Readers who think that Parliament is hampered by its adherence to too many traditional procedures may be surprised to learn of this freedom. It may be that the very freedom to change makes us over-careful of change. The virtue of the British constitution is its flexibility: it can be bent without breaking.

The Constitution of the United States embodies the principle of 'the separation of powers'; that is, it provides that the Executive (the President and his Ministers) shall be separate from the Legislature (Congress, which includes the Senate and the House of Representatives), and the Judiciary (the Judges in the Supreme Court). The idea came from a French writer Montesquieu, who thought that to safeguard individual liberty it was necessary to avoid the concentration of governmental power into one hand (as in France before the revolution). He therefore recommended 'the separation of power', and quoted England as an example of where it existed. It may have been true when he wrote (1731): it is certainly not true of Britain today.

In the United States, the President is elected separately from the Members of Congress. He chooses his Ministers from *outside* Congress. He has to get his Bills and his Budget passed by Congress in which his party may be in a minority. He may well have less power than a British Prime Minister, who has been chosen, not directly by the people's vote, but by the members of the largest party in the House of Commons. The Prime Minister is usually in command of a majority in the Commons: and the Members of his Cabinet are drawn from Parliament and answerable to it. In Britain, then, the Executive (the Cabinet) and the Legislature are closely linked and the Executive usually has power there. This, we think, makes for more effective government — though probably a citizen of the United States of America would not agree.

One aspect of the United States system might be worth adopting here. Parliamentary candidates are chosen by the local party caucus or inner committee, in some cases a very small group. In the USA the electors are brought in at this stage in the Primary Elections. Supporters of each party register themselves as such and have the opportunity, in the primaries, to select their party candidate. It is argued by some people that the British method is better because a small group may well be able to look into the qualities of a candidate more searchingly than the general public whose impressions are inevitably superficial.

10.2 Dictatorship

It is difficult for anyone who has grown up since the Second World War to believe that in the inter-war years some important newspapers and a number of influential people in this country spoke and wrote approvingly of dictatorship. For a while there was a small, but noisy party advocating it. Because it may become an issue again (if, for example, there were to be a world economic recession and prolonged mass unemployment), it is as well to review the arguments for and against.

In the 1930s there were 3 million unemployed in this country, 6 million in Germany and 15 million in the USA. We were suffering from a world-wide depression from which we seemed unable to escape. None of the political parties was able to find the answer. By contrast, Mussolini — a dictator — in Italy, was 'making his trains run on time'; strikes that had paralysed Italian industry after the First World War had been outlawed and trade unions suppressed. The Italian people were alive and hopeful as Mussolini's empire expanded from North Africa into Abyssinia. Outside Rome the Pontine Marshes were drained and in Libya agricultural settlements provided land for Italy's pressing population. In Germany, Hitler took over a defeated nation, impoverished by a harsh peace settlement, its middle class reduced to ruin by inflation; and suffering worse economic dislocation than Britain. He promised escape from defeat and depression, the restoration of Germany's strength and the return of German people to the Fatherland. The German people voted him in: he suspended Parliamentary government, recruited the unemployed in a Labour Corps and a semi-military organisation to combat political opposition, and as he rearmed, industry and trade expanded and unemployment vanished. Youth was organised. Germany was on the march.

Meanwhile, we seemed stuck in the mud. It was natural, therefore, that some people should look to dictatorship as a way out for this country. Dictatorship did seem to have practical advantages over democracies. Decisions could be made rapidly, whereas Parliament was said to be a mere talking shop. Every democratic country was a battleground of warring groups; dictator countries were unified, their peoples marching shoulder to shoulder.

Supporters of democracy drew on the experience of history: dictators, they urged, only tolerated 'yes-men' in their inner councils. Anyone prepared to stand up to them — any prospective rival — was liquidated. Inevitably dictators came to think of themselves as supermen, eventually as gods. Then they destroyed themselves and their people. Hitler and Mussolini unified their people, it was true, but only by destroying opposition. Socialists, Communists and Liberals were the first to be put into concentration camps. The dictators roused enthusiasm by preaching an exclusive nationalism, continually threatening other nations and won victory after victory without actual war. Hitler preached a crude race doctrine and turned his people's frustrations against the Jews, of whom he murdered 6 million. The people were no longer required to think about politics and make political decisions. They enjoyed bread and circuses: great national rallies, local festivities, bands, trips on the river. But inevitably the dictators took their people into war. Millions died. Their countries were devastated. This time they were not subjected to a crushing 'peace' settlement but were helped to re-establish a democratic way of life: starting up the difficult business of running their own affairs.

Not all dictatorships have led their peoples into wars. Some, like that in Portugal, were not powerful enough to do so, and concentrated on internal affairs. Nor can the Russian dictatorship under Stalin, be said to have launched a world war of conquest. True, Soviet Russia seized bordering countries in 1939 as a cushion to protect its boundaries: and in 1945 pushed forward again, installing puppet régimes on its borders. Since Stalin's death, Russia has been ruled by a party oligarchy, that is, a small group of Communist Party leaders. Changes in the composition of this group have occurred from time to time — some, such as Khruschev have been 'retired', but rule by a small group continues.

10.3 People's democracies

Russia and her neighbouring Communist States call themselves 'People's Democracies'. Is this a sour joke? Can a country that permits only one party be a democracy? Communists explain that parties represent classes. When the capitalist class in Russia was abolished by the revolution in 1917 one class only remained, the working class. The Communist Party was its party and expressed its wishes. Since the introduction of the Stalin constitution of 1926 every adult citizen has had a vote. There is direct election to the Supreme Soviet (or Committee) which meets from time to time and selects the Praesidium, or Executive, which is the real repository of power. Four-fifths of the members of the Supreme Soviet are members of the Communist Party, the others independents. There are local soviets, national soviets, factory and farm soviets. There are trade unions and organisations of writers, musicians and other cultural workers. Through all these organisations, it is said, the individual can play his part, voice his objections, exert his influence. Supporters of the communist idea say that this gives more real democracy (or 'government by the people') than exists in say the United States of America or Britain, where wealthy people and business corporations are said to hold the real power.

Opponents of the communist view say that in communist countries power is in fact concentrated in the Communist Party and particularly the leaders who effectively control nominations and elections at all levels: that the oligarchy in control of the State and party also controls newspapers, radio and television: the armed forces, the police, the judiciary; and above all the education system: that there is no debate on public policy, especially on the larger issues, except in the inner counsels of party and State: and that in consequence, there is no democracy.

Under its oligarchic leadership Russia appears to be moving towards a freer form of society. The secret police, formerly under Beria, who disappeared in the early days of the oligarchy, have been curbed. Discussion of economic policy in terms that would not have been permitted under Stalin is now encouraged. Critics do not just disappear. Writers can criticise Soviet life and institutions — up to a point. There is less interference with the work of painters and musicians. Since the crisis over Cuba, there has been no military probing overseas and the leaders of Russia appear anxious to pursue 'peaceful coexistence'. However, it is clear, since the invasion and military occupation of Czechoslovakia in 1968, that it will not permit the liberalising process to go 'too far', even in a satellite. Going too far involves the freedom of press and radio to criticise communist policy and practices and advocate greater independence from Soviet influence. Russia claims that it was called in to preserve the revolution, threatened by groups wishing to restore capitalism, if necessary by force of arms. Alternatively it claims that the occupation was militarily necessary to strengthen Czechoslovakia against Federal Germany and her NATO allies. The fact that the communist parties in most western countries condemned the Russian action in Czechoslovakia, where they saw moves towards liberalisation as a hopeful trend, reduces the persuasiveness of the Soviet case.

10.4 France: the fifth republic

The French system of government established by General de Gaulle is a modified democracy: it arose out of France's excessively fragmented party system of the inter-war and early post-war years. Its too-political electorate opted for a range of political parties from near-fascist on the

Some people are mystified by the terms 'Right' and 'Left' in politics. They arose from a traditional semi-circular seating arrangement in many Continental Parliaments where there are often many parties. Thus:

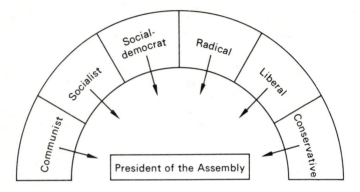

'Left' of the President are the Communists. 'Right' of the President are the Conservatives. The rest shade off in between.

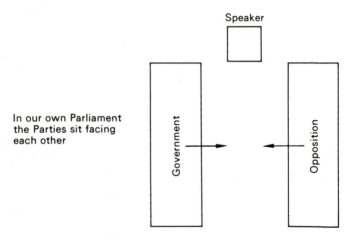

In our own Parliament the Parties sit facing each other

(see diagram of House of Commons on p. 52)

It is sometimes said that the Continental arrangements for seating encourages the many-party system; ours the two-party system.

Fig. 8 'Right' and 'Left' in politics

extreme right, through conservative, liberal, radical to moderate socialist and communist on the extreme left. ('Right' and 'Left' as labels for the parties arises from the seating in the French chamber where the Deputies sit in a semi-circle with the communists physically on the left and the near-fascists on the right. See diag. opposite.) None of these parties was able to get a majority at a general election: accordingly, a succession of unstable coalitions held office. When a measure distasteful to one of the parties in the coalition was proposed, that party would secede: the rump of the coalition would no longer have a majority in the Chamber and the government would fall. A new coalition, moved slightly to the right or left, would succeed with an equally unstable existence. In these circumstances there was no firm government; unpopular decisions were shirked. General de Gaulle, who after the fall of France in 1940 had been the symbol of France's struggle against Germany, had returned in triumph at the end of the war. In 1946, having set up the Fourth Republic, he retired with the status of an elder statesman. In 1958 he was called back to deal with the threatened disintegration of France, following some disastrous colonial wars and rumours of army intervention in metropolitan France. He brought in a new constitution ('The Fifth Republic') under which, as President, he had greatly increased powers. He appointed the Prime Minister and government. Parliament, though still elected on a 'one man, one vote' basis, had limited powers. It is difficult to put this form of government into a specific category. It is by no means an absolute dictatorship because there is a democratically elected Parliament at its base; and the President is elected for seven years only. It has been described as an absolute, but beneficial monarchy, so organised that when the 'monarch' is a strong personality, like General de Gaulle, he can get his way: whereas a less dominating person with a strong Prime Minister would have no more political power than, say, the Queen of England.

10.5 Some former colonial countries

Many African and Asian countries, on securing independence from colonial rule, began with democratic Parliamentary institutions like those of their former mother countries — a neat compliment, incidentally, to their former rulers. Many are still operating those constitutions. It is a mistake to think that all have broken down. India, for example, the largest, continues. But trouble gets more publicity than success and it is understandable that the impression of failure gains currency. Among the 'failures' is Ghana, on the west coast of Africa, which began with a Parliamentary constitution worked out in amicable agreement with the British and launched in the presence of British Royalty. President Nkrumah was hailed as his country's saviour and was indeed the architect of its freedom. But he and his National Convention People's Party sought to centralise power in their own hands. Youth movements, labour corps, trade unions, producers' organisations, churches came under their control. Opposition leaders were arrested on charges of conspiring to murder Nkrumah. Even members of the Cabinet were deposed and imprisoned. Huge public works were put in hand, such as the electricity generating system at Tema, on the River Volta. But resources also were poured out on prestige buildings like hotels and conference halls, and houses for the leader. Nkrumah now appeared very like a dictator being given, if not demanding, godlike status. As reserves of foreign currency ran out and evidence of corruption and inefficiency mounted, the army staged a revolt in Nkrumah's absence in 1966 and the country was then run by a military oligarchy the basis of which was gradually broadened by the inclusion of former opposition leaders: and in 1969 a general election brought a new, popularly elected government to power.

Nigeria presents a different picture. It was one of the largest and wealthiest African colonies; it had secured independence with little violence; there were established parties and politicians in all the areas: accordingly much was hoped of it. It was set up as a federation: four regions with differing history, religion and tribal organisation were each given their own Parliaments for the conduct of local affairs. At the centre was a Federal Parliament to govern Nigeria as a whole. The army was answerable to the federal government and was called into the regions from time to time when political rivalries led to a breakdown of order or when the federal government decided to intervene in a region's affairs. The Federation held together precariously until 1966 when the army took over. A number of political leaders were murdered, including the Federal Prime Minister, Sir Abubakar Tafawa Balewa, KBE, a Muslim from the northern, dominant region. His assassins were thought to be Ibo army officers from the eastern region. The Ibos, who had spread throughout the whole of Nigeria and particularly into the Muslim north, were energetic, intelligent and western educated. They had become prominent in government service and in business and were unpopular. A massacre of Ibos resident in the northern region took place, probably in revenge for the murder of the Federal Prime Minister. The surviving Ibos crowded back into the eastern region which declared itself independent under General Odjukwu and renamed itself Biafra. This region, which was not exclusively Ibo, contained much of the mineral wealth — and particularly the oil — of Nigeria.

The federal government sent troops to put down this rebellion and civil war followed. Ultimately the Biafran forces were defeated.

Meanwhile the four large regions were divided into twelve smaller but more homogeneous areas, of which one was Iboland, in a new federation still under the control of the army, but with politicians being brought in to widen the basis of government.

What can be said for or against these military régimes? How long are they likely to last? (There are long-established military régimes in Egypt, Pakistan and the Sudan.) Frequently they restore order and discipline where anarchy and corruption had hitherto reigned. Educated (in military matters), disciplined and incorruptible as many of them are, the military leaders frequently do not understand the economic and political problems that underlie their countries' difficulties. The wiser of them rely on their civil servants for technical advice and bring in the more trustworthy political leaders so that gradually the régime is broadened. The more flamboyant engage in military adventures. The great drawback of this form of government is that there is no constitutional way to get rid of an unwanted leader. One of democracy's greatest assets is that it provides the means of peaceful change.

10.6 Controlling the military

The experience of these African countries highlights one of the oldest problems of government: how to maintain civilian control of the armed forces. In the settled countries of the West, there is a long tradition of civilian control. The last time Britain faced trouble was in 1914 when the officers at the Curragh, in Ulster (now Northern Ireland), threatened mutiny if the Liberal government went on with its plan for Irish Home Rule. The outbreak of war in Europe closed the issue. The French army (as noted above) threatened intervention in political affairs in 1958. In May 1968, when the students of Paris were in revolt and the trade unions staged sit-in strikes in the factories, there were signs that General de Gaulle's régime might fall. The General, unknown to the people, flew to all the French military headquarters and found that they were firmly behind him: he returned to Paris, promised firm action against any further disorders, negotiated a settlement with the unions and greater participation for the students. Had he found disaffection among the army, history might have been very different.

The United States war hero General MacArthur threatened to disobey orders in the Korean War and attack China, but 'the little guy', President Truman, flew to Korea and fired him. Is there a danger that the huge military complex in the United States (known collectively as The Pentagon, from the building housing its headquarters) might ever take over? It controls a large part of the budget and directs millions of dollars into industry, research, the universities and intelligence. If there were a serious economic collapse and the breakdown of order it might do so. Any military organisation is a potential power in the State and can exert pressures. Even in Russia, where the army is subject to control by political commissars, it has its representatives in the Praesidium. It is possible that the invasion of Czechoslovakia in 1968 was due to military, as much as to political, pressures. Israel's external policy is patently influenced by its armed forces. In Hitler's Germany the military general staff was probably a restraining influence: in the Kaiser's Germany it was an influence for war.

Summing up, we see that it is an over-simplification to speak of any government simply as democratic or autocratic or a military dictatorship. Power does not often lie in the hands of a single group, even in a dictatorship. In a democracy there are many centres of power, political, economic, military, which hold one another in check. It is necessary to examine the institutions of a country and the balance of forces there to assess where real power lies and particularly before one can say of it that it has government of, by and for the people.

Questions *for discussion and action*
1. 'Dictatorship! It can't happen here.'

    Consider the circumstances in which Parliamentary democracy as we have it in Britain might break down and suggest the form that a new system of government to replace it, might take.
2. Can a 'one-party' state be democratic?

    Ask the representative of a one-party state like Zambia to speak to the group on the difficulties in his country, for example, of tribalism, which make for divisions within the nation.

    Ask a representative from a State that is currently unpopular; for example, Uganda, to talk to the group about its problems and policies.
3. In the 'trouble' in Northern Ireland in the early 1970s the Army was called in to support the local police and restore 'law and order'. At first the troops were popular with both sides who looked on them as protectors. Later they became unpopular. Why?

    Should the Army ever be used for law-and-order purposes?
4. Examine the newspapers for evidence supporting or disproving the statement made above that 'Israel's external policy is patently influenced by its armed forces'.

Part 2

Party politics and the people

Chapter 11

Party politics: necessary or unnecessary ?

Nowadays, people are deeply cynical about politics, especially party politics. This is probably because they do not understand the job it has to do.

Parties have developed in this country as our Parliamentary system has developed. They have an essential part to play in it. There are, of course, times when our politicians do their job badly. They should be criticised for that. What we should not do is dismiss party politics as unnecessary or beneath the contempt of reasonable people.

11.1 The case for party politics

First, Parliamentary government could not continue to function in its present form unless there were an organised and disciplined party behind the government. Further, it would be far less efficient if there were no organised opposition to keep the government on its toes.

Second, the parties work out policies. Each party has a wide spread of opinion within its ranks but collectively it presents a policy that has a certain unity: it holds together. Most of its members can accept most of it. It presents the issues to the electorate in terms that can be understood. These policies are subjected to the criticism of the opposing parties.

Third, the parties provide alternative governments: they train up and have ready groups of men and women who can take over the reins of government should the existing group be rejected by the electorate.

Fourth, and probably this is the most important purpose: parties represent 'interests'. Party politics is the means by which claims are asserted and settlements arrived at. Parliament provides the arena in which 'the battle of the interests' is fought.

Finally, parties provide opportunities for citizens to participate effectively in local and national affairs.

11.2 Organising Parliamentary business

A careful reading of the Parliamentary report in one of the more serious newspapers such as *The Times, Guardian* or *Daily Telegraph* or of *Hansard* (the daily report of the proceedings of the House of Commons) will illustrate the first point. Parties are needed to organise the business of the House. Time is short and eagerly sought in the Commons. Each day, except Friday, begins with Question Time, when Ministers attend to answer questions put to them in writing and to answer supplementary questions, an important time for challenging government action and keeping Ministers in touch with public feeling (see p. 60). The remaining time must be tightly organised. In a typical week in April 1972 the following business was completed:

House of Commons

Monday, 17 April 1972. Statement on the Rail Dispute and Govan Shipbuilders Ltd. Local Government Bill further considered on report. Money resolution for Housing (Financial Provisions) (Scotland) Bill. Adjournment debate about workers' shares in the old Rolls-Royce Company. House adjourned 12.2 am (Tuesday).

Tuesday, 18 April 1972. Derby Corporation, Reigate Congregational Church, Solihull Corporation and Sunderland Corporation Bills read a third time. Harbours, Piers and Ferries (Scotland) Bill read first time. European Communities Bill further considered in Committee. Adjournment debate about curtailment of the teachers' special recruitment scheme in Scotland. House adjourned 3.47 am (Wednesday).

Wednesday, 19 April 1972. Statements on the Rail Dispute and the Widgery Tribunal Report. Congregational Chapel and Trust Property Deptford Bill read first time. European Communities Bill considered further in Committee. Adjournment debate about government policy on docks, waterways and river quays in and around Goole. House adjourned 2.27 am (Thursday).

Thursday, 20 April 1972. Finance Bill read second time by 292 votes to 258. Consolidated Fund (No. 3) Bill read second time. International Institute for the Management of Technology and Interim Commission for the International Trade Organisation (Immunities and Privileges) Orders approved. Betting and Gaming Duties Bill passed Committee stage. Adjournment debate about appointment of women to public boards. House adjourned 11.26 pm

Friday, 21 April 1972. National Insurance (Amendment) and Sunday Theatre (No. 2) Bills passed remaining stages. Control of Personal Information Bill considered on second reading, adjourned. Adjournment debate about fog walls and planning motorway routes. House adjourned 4.34 pm.

The main items in the programme are arranged the previous week by the Leader of the House on the government side and the Chief Whip on the opposition side — what are known as 'the usual channels'. Immediately after Question Time on Thursdays, the Leader of the House announces the broad programme for the ensuing week. Immediately, Members from all sides rise to ask for time to discuss matters in which they are particularly interested. The first asks for time to debate 'the heavy unemployment figures announced today', the second the threatened railway stoppage. Another wishes to discuss 'the critically important question of land prices, house prices and land for housing', another asks for a full day, not a half day as announced, for the Museums and Galleries Admission Charges Bill. An Ulster Member wants a debate on the deteriorating situation in Northern Ireland. A Tyneside Member wants a statement about a large engineering works in her constituency where redundancies are threatened. Scottish Members are concerned about the proposal to reform local government in Scotland. A Member asks about the withholding of the special Social Security fuel allowance from one of his pensioner constituents; another wants information about a commonwealth island in the Caribbean where riots have been reported, and when can he have a debate?

The Leader of the House (chosen for his tact) agrees that these are important questions: no one would be more pleased than he if an extra day could be found next week — or indeed every week — to discuss them. In fact, very little time is made available but Members are given suggestions about when they can raise the subjects during set debates on Estimates, at normal Question Time and in 'debates on the adjournment'.

It will be seen that a government can get through its programme of legislation and provide time for important discussions only if the business of the House is tightly organised. And it is not only the business in the debating chamber but of many specialist committees sitting simultaneously. If there were no parties but 630 independent MPs each seeking his own ends, there would be chaos. Some people complain that our (predominantly) two-party system does not give sufficient choice of party to the citizen with independent views. The experience of France under the Third and Fourth Republics with their multi-party system is a sufficient warning. The parties there were too small to govern alone and linked up with others to form coalition governments. These proved very unstable and quickly fell apart, to be replaced by yet another coalition. At least, the two-party system makes possible the efficient dispatch of business. Members complain that they are kept on a tight rein by the Whips and pressed to vote on issues where they may have doubts. This seems unavoidable in view of the press of business and, provided that there is always opportunity for abstention on grounds of principle, not insupportable.

At one stage the Liberals, with a dozen Members, were claiming that their Members were the only free men in the House, able to vote as intelligence and conscience directed: and were obviously the ones for whom the electorate should vote. Their 'freedom' however is a luxury dependent on their insignificance: on the day they become a potential government or official opposition their Whips will come into play. Parties and party discipline are essential today if Parliament is to work.

11.3 Representing interests

But however important this function is, it is not the main function of the political parties. The parties were formed to press the views and interests of a particular section of the British people. They seek power for this purpose. Parliament provides an arena in which 'the battle of the interests' is fought: where an accommodation is reached. This is a far more civilised way of settling differences than at the barricades.

Let us examine these 'interests'.

In any society where people are free to live their own lives there will be considerable diversity: people will want to get their livings in different ways; some will want to live in the north, some in the south; some in town, some in the country; some will want to be their own bosses, some will be content to work for others — and of course, for most there will be no choice except as between one boss and another. Some people will want to buy their own houses, others to live in council houses or flats; some will want their children to attend private schools, others not; some will be churchgoers, or car owners or pub crawlers — others not. And in order to further their interests in these capacities, many people will be members of organisations specially formed for these purposes: trade unions, employers' associations, professional bodies like the British Medical Association (the doctors' organisation), shopkeepers' or farmers' associations; ex-servicemen's clubs, parent—teacher associations, churches, local councils for social service, welfare organisations for old people, neglected children, unmarried mothers and so on; even old age pensioners' associations.

Political parties are similar 'pressure' organisations but on a wider basis. Each party embraces a range of interests, more or less compatible. Thus, on the whole farmers and businessmen will support the Conservative Party and in turn expect its support. The trade unions support the Labour Party. Nevertheless, many working-class people vote Conservative and a substantial percentage of middle- and upper-class people vote Labour. This is because the parties have developed policies aimed at a wide section of the electorate — have sought to avoid a narrow class appeal. Indeed, all parties now claim to represent 'the national interest'. The fact is, though, that most of the decisions made by governments affect group interests, even when they cover everyone in the country; for example, a law compelling all children to go to State schools would affect those now going to private schools quite differently from those already going to State schools.

Many of the clashes between 'interests' occur outside Parliament, many in the ordinary course of economic life. Trade unions dispute with employers. In far and away the greater number of cases settlements are arrived at — though not before much hard bargaining has taken place. In some disputes deadlock occurs — a strike or lock-out is called to bring pressure to bear, until the sides come together in a compromise or with one party victorious. Similarly the steel industry bargains with the coal industry over the price of fuel; farmers want a higher price for meat and negotiate with the wholesale butchers who, in turn, squeeze the retailers. The housewife decides that beef is too dear and goes in for lamb and chicken. All this is outside Parliament, but Parliament nevertheless influences even these contests.

Firstly, Parliament holds the ring. Acts of Parliament, passed over a long period of time, determine what can or cannot be done by a trade union and what can be done in a strike. Limitations are put on wage claims in times of 'squeeze and freeze'. The 'shape' of the contestants is also affected by government policy. At a time of full-employment — the result of government policies — both trade unions and employers will be in different positions of strength from those in periods of mass-unemployment. Employers also may benefit from grants or tax concessions to help them install new machinery, thereby increasing output and their ability to meet wage-demands. The government may enter the ring, as with negotiations over teachers' or doctors' pay or in the annual agreement on farm prices and subsidies. Or it may appear as a backer when the dispute is between British Rail and the railwaymen and special arrangements are made to enable the railways to meet the railwaymen's claims.

An interesting example of the government adjudicating between contesting interests occurred in March 1968 following the disastrous foot and mouth disease epidemic when thousands of infected cattle were slaughtered and burnt. Farmers wanted imports of all types of meat from the Argentine banned on the grounds that they were a possible source of contamination. The government could not overlook the fact that Argentine meat was a competitor with English meat: banning Argentine meat would leave the market to English farmers; meat would be scarce and high in price. This might be good for the farmer but unfair to the consumer. Then the butchers' representatives spoke up. There was no proof, they said, that the beef from the Argentine was contaminated, only the lamb. Furthermore, British farmers could not possibly increase the supply of beef to make up for the Argentine beef. Another group now came on the scene: exporters to the Argentine. If we cut off *all* imports from the Argentine, they said, the Argentine would stop taking our exports. The government weighed up the evidence and considered the competing claims. It decided to ban Argentine mutton and lamb but permit beef to come in.

Apart from its influence in economic and industrial disputes, the government plays another role: it acts to equalise the distribution of wealth by taxation and through social welfare schemes. Thus, people who are at work pay in each week so that those who are out of work receive unemployment pay and do not fall below a minimum standard of existence. Those who are well support those who are ill — through National Insurance and the Health Service. People of working age support those who are too old to work, or too young. Taxation ensures that the burden falls more heavily on the rich than the poor. The government is also expected to help financially in times of natural disaster: a flood in Cornwall, a hurricane in Glasgow, the fouling of beaches following the Torrey Canyon wreck. The 'claims' of people in distress are met by the rest of us.

What is done on all these occasions will depend on the government in power. Governments do not, in fact, see eye-to-eye on these matters: they settle the claims, they redistribute the nation's wealth, in different ways. How they see the problem is discussed in the following chapters on party policies. The point here is that government provides a means for weighing claims and their settlement. The more varied and interesting a society, the more rapidly it is in process of change, the greater the need for politics. Party government gives the contestants — that is, all of us — a share in the decisions.

A share, yes, it may be protested, but not an equal share. Many people, often those in greatest need, do not know how to bring pressure: many groups (for example, the mentally ill or homeless or fatherless) by their very nature cannot exert pressure to secure their interests.

Again, it may be protested, the system does not settle questions on their merits but on the strengths of the pressures exerted. The man who shouts the loudest (or can hold up production or bring the docks to a halt) gets away with it.

Further, are not some interests so powerful that they are the real governors in the land? Some Conservatives think that the trade unions are excessively powerful. They think that the government should limit their powers. Some socialists, on the other hand, think that big business interests, international financiers and multinational corporations are the source of danger — a challenge to government authority.

Ian Gilmour, MP, a moderate Conservative commentator [1], discounts the view that these interests are sinister and dangerous. Noting that there are about 1,300 organised manufacturing associations, 2,500 trade associations and nearly 600 trade unions (of which only 170 are affiliated to the Trades Union Congress), he sees them as useful channels of information and convenient sources of consultation between themselves, representing sectional interests, and the government as adjudicator.

How strong are these bodies, vis-à-vis the government?

On closer examination 'the trade unions' do not look excessively powerful. Of course, they are more powerful in prolonged periods of full employment than they were in the inter-war years of mass unemployment. But they are not a united body — rather a group of bodies pursuing separate and often competing interests. The Trades Union Congress General Council, though speaking in the name of the trade union movement, has very limited powers. It sometimes receives contradictory instructions from its annual Congress. Some people, indeed, think it should have more power to commit its member unions. But the unions themselves, although some have great economic power in their ability to hold up economic activity, cannot (and do not choose) to take the nation to the point of economic breakdown. The unions' challenge to the government over the Industrial Relations Bill was confined to demonstrations and one-day strikes. The extremists who called for a general strike, not just for one day, but until the government surrendered, were completely unrepresentative (though given much publicity on television). The unions accepted the 'freeze' on wages under both the Labour and Conservative governments. (See Chapter 15.) Once it was the law of the land, they accepted 'restraint'. We, including the majority of trade unionists, are a law-abiding people. True, by too great a concentration on sectional interests they may promote inflation and threaten the whole economy. But they do not see it this way. They are 'protecting their members' interests'. Few, if any, promote inflation as a conscious revolutionary aim.

The power of the trade union movement is considerable: but, it may be argued, so it should be, representing so large and necessary a part of the nation. So long as it seeks to influence, but not to replace, the government, it is not a constitutional threat.

Similarly with 'big business'. Here again, there are competing interests, and the collective organisation, the Confederation of British Industry, is not itself a powerful body. It can rarely pledge the support of all its members. But could not enough big businessmen 'go on strike', reduce production, create massive unemployment and so undermine a government it sought to remove? Do not international financiers put pressure on unpopular governments by 'runs on the £' or 'pressure on the dollar'?

A determined government has many weapons in its armoury: nationalisation, embargoes on the export of capital, control of imports. The large business corporations also have an interest in the country as a going concern.

In a democratic country power is not concentrated: competing centres of power hold one another in check. This system of 'countervailing' power enables a government (provided it is not to be bullied) to make the final decisions, to adjudicate between the interests.

There is need for constant vigilance so that we can know who is putting on the pressure. There may be sinister elements in the trade unions; apparently disinterested organisations may be a 'front' for powerful business interests. Large sums may be spent on publicity in favour of a road here or an airport there. It is essential that we know who puts up the money. Our newspapers expose much of this activity: it rests with us whether or not we use the information they supply.

11.4 Opportunities for the citizen 'to take part'

Politics, in fact, enables us to 'run our own affairs'. Not everyone, of course, wants to take part either in party or local politics. (Those who don't, though, should not grumble if their views — and interests — are not considered.)

In Part 1, 'You and your government', we set out some of the activities undertaken by party members at election time. Many people who normally take no part in politics join in then. There is the heightened interest generated by newspapers and radio coverage, the sporting element in the contest. But election activity is by no means the most important political work to be done especially at local level.

The larger parties are organised on a constituency basis — there is for example in the London Borough of Camden, Hampstead constituency, a Hampstead Conservative and Unionist Association, a Hampstead Labour Party, a Hampstead Liberal Party. These are broken down into ward sections, covering each of the seven wards in this part (the Hampstead part) of the Borough of Camden. The ward parties organise meetings for their members. Each month there may be a business meeting, a discussion, a social, a canvassing evening and a working party preparing for the annual bazaar. Not all members will attend all these activities. At the discussions a speaker may open up on a topic like 'Britain and the European Economic Community Today' or 'Incomes Policy' or 'A new look at Housing' or 'Hampstead and the proposed Motorway Box', and Members put their views. Usually this is looked upon as a purely educational activity and no vote is taken but it may result in a 'resolution' being put forward at the next ward business meeting. (A resolution is an expression of opinion usually coupled with a demand for action.) Thus, Adelaide Ward of the . . . . Party might put forward to the Hampstead Party a resolution in the form 'That the Hampstead . . . . Party objects strongly to the proposed Box Motor Road on the grounds that it will destroy the amenities of the area, take away the homes of many hundreds of citizens and provide no solution to the traffic problem. It calls on the Party's representatives on the Camden Borough Council, the Greater London Council and in Parliament to take all possible steps to stop the proposal.'

If this resolution is passed by the ward, it will come before the next meeting of the borough party at which all the wards are represented. Discussion will follow — a vote be taken. If it is passed, the secretary of the borough party will write to the councillors involved, Camden party, the London party, and the Parliamentary party as necessary and will no doubt receive replies.

This action illustrates the function of parties to act as a channel for information to be passed up from the rank-and-file members to the representatives at various levels: and for information to come down from the party leadership to the active local membership. It also illustrates the process of party education.

Sometimes the local parties take more 'direct action'. They may demonstrate in a shopping centre against rising prices, join a protest by flat-dwellers against unsatisfactory housing, organise a parade of angry mothers for the provision of a zebra-crossing. Some have succeeded in getting the gardens in residential squares open to the public: others have converted derelict bomb-sites into adventure playgrounds or rest gardens. Sometimes house-to-house inquiries are undertaken to find out what amenities are needed locally — seats for old people, waste-paper baskets, trees, flower-tubs: sometimes just to find house-bound or friendless neighbours who can be put in touch with the council's welfare services.

What sort of people take part?

Many of them are young people — say from about sixteen to twenty-five years of age, some students in the sixth forms of secondary schools where current issues are being discussed, or at college or university where political societies and union debates stimulate interest. Most parties provide a special organisation (Young Socialists, Young Conservatives, Young Liberals, etc.) where the younger members can meet for their own political, educational and social purposes, but they are also encouraged to be individual members of the parent party so that they do not become too isolated. (There is a tendency for the Youth Section to be more extreme than the parent body!) Youth sections usually have their representatives on the parent body so that they can take their views direct as well as through the wards where they are members. They stir up — and sometimes exasperate — the older members who may well become complacent as they see reforms for which they have worked (in education, in council rents policy, in old people's welfare) become accepted policy. These are taken for granted by the younger members who are then way ahead on other trails.

Local party activities are not confined to education and propaganda. A member soon finds that he (or, equally, she) is invited to become a member of the management committee of a local primary school, or a governor of a secondary school or technical college; to become a co-opted member of a committee overseeing the council's residential or day-nurseries, old people's homes, residential hostels or community homes. This is good work for those who are not particularly interested in 'politics' but are 'good with people'. They bring their practical common sense to bear on the running of these institutions: represent the view of ordinary people.

Local parties provide other opportunities for people who 'want to get things done'. Members may become magistrates, or go as party representatives to the local branch of the Workers' Education Association, the United Nations' Association, the Association for the Advancement of State Education, the local Consumers' group, the Ramblers' Association (who 'walk' public footpaths to keep open rights of way), the local branch of the Council for the Preservation of Rural England, the National Playing Fields Association, the National Council for the Unmarried Mother and her Child, many of them supported by Left and Right in politics.

Members who are interested in local affairs — and have shown their interest in activities such as those mentioned — will be welcome as party candidates for election to borough and county councils: there are rarely enough suitable candidates coming forward. They will have to inform themselves pretty thoroughly on the scope of local government, on what has or has not been done locally and on pressing local issues. The party's programme is (theoretically) the collective effort of all the candidates but in practice the distilled wisdom of the previous councillors and their party advisers. Candidates appear at public meetings, speak briefly and invite questions. Some of them will be elected. Perhaps the party will be the 'majority party' on the local council, that is, have more councillors than the other parties. Then their representatives will have the responsibility of 'running' the council. They will supply the chairmen of the committees and formulate policy. Every councillor will be a member of one or more committees and be expected to specialise in its work. The main committees look after Housing; Health; Social Services; Planning and Communications; Leisure Services; Buildings and Works; Finance and General Purposes; Policy and Resources; and Staff and Management. It will be seen that a vast area is covered: indeed, it has been said that the councils are concerned with our lives from the cradle to the grave. The quality of local life depends very much on the activities of the council and it is important that good people volunteer to take part: the work is unpaid and requires the sacrifice of a good deal of time but is very rewarding. The parties want the best people they can find to represent them: not only people who can make rousing speeches but good administrators with human sympathies and imagination. This is particularly suitable work for the younger middle-aged — say the thirty to thirty-five year olds — but this does not exclude the twenty year olds from making a start at it.

For people with more exalted political ambitions work on the council is a useful apprenticeship. The man or woman who wishes to become a Member of Parliament will get his name on the list of party candidates: anyone who is active in local politics will let his friends know and they will nominate him. The list is circulated to party branches throughout the country. The prospective candidate will, perhaps, be sent by his local party to the annual national conference of the party. He will speak on a subject he particularly cares about and may be seen on TV or his photograph may be in the newspapers. Thereafter he may be called to a selection meeting in a not very hopeful constituency and chosen from half a dozen others to be their prospective Parliamentary candidate. After one or two elections at which he makes a good showing and increases the party vote he may be invited to stand for a marginal constituency; and if the country is swinging towards his party he will become its Member of Parliament.

It may be objected that the foregoing gives an idealised view of local party activity: that many local parties are moribund or engaged in bitter feuds or provide opportunities for busy-bodies and place seekers. Of course, there are people like that in all parties, just as there are in churches and clubs and other organisations: that does not deny the value of these organisations. Not all the activities described will be found in every party but all will be found somewhere among them.

None of this will appeal to the person who wants to sit in front of his television every night, turning it off every time public affairs are mentioned. It is for the more active, usually younger and more socially aware. Some people take up politics for the sheer interest of it. Others are pushed into it because of something that happens to them: their house is pulled down to make way for luxury flats, the local school is being closed or turned 'comprehensive', there aren't enough children's nurseries, their children are getting into trouble for lack of local play facilities. Others are shocked into it by a war or the horror of the atom bomb. Others, quieter but no less dedicated, want to 'do something for others' or 'to leave the world a better place'. Whatever the reason, the individual's participation enriches democracy. Indeed, it can hardly be said to *be* democracy if it is only of the people and for the people: it must also be 'by the people' if Abraham Lincoln's definition is to mean anything.

Questions *for discussion and action*

1. Mention some of the organisations (such as trade unions, sports associations, consumer groups) which exist to further interests in which you share. Say if you are active in any of them. Could you participate more in their activities? Do you think that they are *(a)* little, *(b)* moderately, *(c)* greatly, effective?

2. Refer to *Hansard* at your public library. Note the business decided on Thursday for the following week. Arrange a visit to the House, or, if this is not practicable, watch the newspapers and next week's *Hansard*, for an account of the debate on any matter in which you are specially interested.

3. It is sometimes said that back-bench Members are little more than 'voting-fodder'. Watch the newspapers for examples of successful pressure by back-bench Members to secure a change of government plans. Some of these result in a free vote being permitted: note the issues involved.

4. Details are given in this chapter of the pressure brought by British farming interests in the matter of Argentine meat imports. Watch for similar incidents. Make a list of the organised interests, or pressure groups involved. Note especially the outcome of these pressures in government action.

5. Watch the correspondence columns of local and national newspapers for letters putting forward the views of particular 'interests' (the parties, pensioners' associations, consumer groups, etc.). Estimate their persuasiveness noting how abuse of opponents, etc., reduces it. Write a letter in support or opposition: or initiate a correspondence on an issue in which you are

interested (e.g. lack of sports, leisure or educational opportunities: lack of parking facilities, improvement in trafic arrangements, re-siting of pedestrian crossings, installation of traffic lights; improvements in public transport).

6. If you are a member of the youth section of a political party give your considered opinion on the following comments:

'Youth sections are a mistake. By throwing the young — and inevitably inexperienced — members together they ensure that they become introverted and narrow in their views. They are not, as supposed, 'advanced' in their views, but mouthpieces for slogans a century out of date, which experience has led the older members to reject. Inevitably they become an embarrassment to the party. Young members should be encouraged to join the parent party where their energy and freshness of outlook can act as a stimulus and contact with more experienced members will help them attain political maturity.'

Chapter 12

Party attitudes: Conservative

People frequently complain that there is no difference between the political parties. 'They all do the same when they get in, whatever they promise beforehand', it is said.

It is true that often, faced with economic difficulties, such as rising unemployment, the failure of exports to pay for imports or rapidly rising prices, governments of both parties act in very much the same way. The fact is that in these circumstances there is very little room for manoeuvre. Nevertheless, there are still very wide differences between the parties, seen, for example, when a new government with fresh energy and enthusiasm begins to put its policy into action: and though it may have to tack before stormy winds, its long-term aims remain.

We shall begin, then, by examining the underlying beliefs and ideals of the parties rather than their detailed policies: in this way we shall see what they would *like*, to do, even if, in some circumstances, they are prevented from doing it. In subsequent chapters we shall examine the economic behaviour of post-war governments of both parties, noting similarities and differences and look for evidence of future trends in response to the pressure of new (and sometimes old) ideas.

But first — party attitudes.

12.1 Order in society

Conservatives have always put the establishment of authority and the maintenance of law and order high on their list of priorities: they are, they say, the basis of all societies. One of the most pungent expressions of this view was made by Thomas Hobbes, about 300 years ago. Writing in *Leviathan* [1], out of his unpleasant experiences in the English Civil War, he made a case for disciplined, authoritarian government. Such is man's nature, said Hobbes, that when his competitiveness for possessions, his fear for their safety and his desire for acclaim are not held in check by firm government, then 'they are in that condition which is called Warre; and such warre is of every man against every man'.

And the consequence?

> In such a condition [said Hobbes] there is no place for Industry; because the fruit thereof is uncertain: and consequently no Culture of the Earth, no Navigation nor use of the commodities that may be imported by Sea; no commodious Building; no Instruments of moving and removing such things as require much force; no Knowledge of the face of the Earth; no account of Time; no Arts; no Letters; no Society; and which is worst of all, continuall feare, and danger of violent death, and the life of man solitary, poore, nasty, brutish and short.

Does this exaggerate? Can it be said to describe the situation any where in the world today? Unfortunately, yes. Examine any area where 'law and order' has broken down: an American city in the grip of race-riots; a Canadian town where the police are on strike; in Southern Italy where the Mafia rules; in the gangster underworld of Chicago, New York or London; in parts of Ulster; in areas where wars — and especially civil wars — are fought. Here, indeed, life is nasty, brutish and short.

How, then, do we avoid these ills? According to Hobbes, by each one of us giving up his power to do as he likes and vesting authority in a 'sovereign power'. The sovereign — not necessarily one person but any established government — will arm itself sufficiently to 'hold us all in awe', that is, to ensure that we are not able to defy the law. The power needed by the sovereign need not be great: in a long settled country like Britain, no more, perhaps, than an unarmed police with troops in the background. In less settled communities the State may require greater power — but progressively less as respect for law and order grows. By yielding up our individual power we gain the benefit of ordered society. Trade and agriculture are possible, wealth accumulates, literature and the arts flourish, society expands. Life is no longer 'solitary, poore, nasty, brutish and short'. At the root of this civilised life is authority and discipline.

A classic example of Hobbes's 'condition of anarchy', the absence of order under authority, still exists in international relations. The nations, especially the big powers, have consistently refused to give up their power to a supranational authority. Each one claims the right to settle its disputes, ultimately by force of arms. Peace is maintained, precariously, by a 'balance of power'. On our experience of the past, say Conservatives, we must maintain our armed power. The Army, Navy and Air Force must be kept at peak efficiency. It will be disastrous to our interests, and the peace of the world, if we withdraw from the Middle East and Asia. If we step out and leave a vacuum then some other power will step in to fill it and the delicate 'balance' will be upset. Always there are expansionist powers probing for weaknesses. In the present international anarchy, arms are vital. Without arms, Britain's security and influence would be nil.

12.2 Society a living organism

Edmund Burke, the Tory philosopher of the late eighteenth century, crystallised many of the ideas that inspire Conservatives today. He mounted a steady opposition to the revolutionary doctrines of his time, putting in their place his own view of society as a living, growing organism. Society grows slowly, as a tree does, adding new branches, shedding others. There must be change, but is must be natural, evolutionary, not violent and destructive.

The State is a partnership to secure the main purposes of life. As these cannot be achieved in one lifetime, their fulfilment links the generations. Each inherits the wisdom of earlier generations, adds its own and passes it on to the future. Institutions created to fulfil these purposes, the monarchy, the great landed families, a representative Parliament, should be preserved. This is by no means a recipe for stagnation. 'There should be a disposition to preserve and an ability to improve.'

Burke was suspicious of abstract ideas like 'the rights of man' (he urged, rather the responsibilities of man), of perfectionist constitutions inspired by the French Revolution. This suspicion of ideologies is echoed by Conservatives today. They suspect theories, especially socialist theories, and prefer to act on experience.

Burke wanted a united nation, the great mass of the people led by 'their proper chieftains', and he wrote: [2].

When great multitudes act together under that great discipline of nature [the nation], I recognise The People ... [but] when you separate the common sort of men from their proper chieftains so as to form them into an adverse army, I no longer know that venerable object called the people in such a disbanded race of deserters and vagabonds.

12.3 One nation

A century later the Tory leader Disraeli took up this idea of a 'united nation'. He saw the country being divided into two nations: [3]

Two nations between whom there is no intercourse and no sympathy; who are as ignorant of each others habits, thoughts and feelings as if they were dwellers in different zones, or inhabitants of different planets; who are formed by a different breeding, are fed by a different food, are ordered by different manners, and are not governed by the same laws. . . . The rich and the poor.

The rich were the rising industrialists who had strengthened their political power following the Reform Act of 1832. Disraeli saw the repeal of the Corn Laws in 1846 as a blow at the 'landed interest' (not only the 'squires of high degree' but the populations of country towns and rural villages) and as an act taken in the interest of industrialists who needed cheap food for their workers. Disraeli challenged his leader, Peel, on this issue, split the Tory Party, but rallied it and later became its leader.

As a later Conservative [4] saw it:

Only in the doctrine that the interests of no one class must predominate did he [Disraeli] see hope of saving England. An active monarchy above all party squabbles, a generous-hearted territorial aristocracy bound by an obligation to their tenants, an enfranchised people — these were the instruments to be used in any true scheme of reform.

In 1867 Disraeli's government gave votes to the town-dwelling working class and over subsequent years, introduced wide ranging social reforms: trade unions were given legal status; factory legislation, regulating hours and conditions of employment, was introduced; education for the masses was made available and compulsory: urban housing conditions were improved and towns made more sanitary. The Tory Party enjoyed the support, throughout this period, of a large section of working-class voters, but these were drawn away in the early twentieth century by the social reform programme of the radical Liberals and later by the new Labour Party; however, something like one-third of the working class still vote Conservative, making up more than half of that party's poll.

12.4 An hierarchical system and the need for leadership

There must be 'one nation'; yes, agree Conservatives. And the interests of no one class must predominate. True. But this is not to advocate a 'classless society', as socialists do. Every society, say Conservatives,

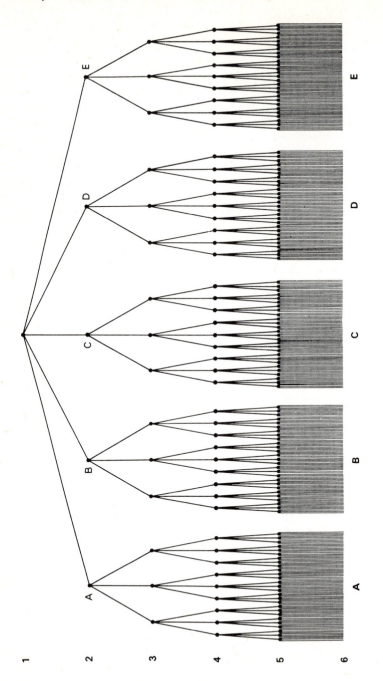

Party attitudes: Conservative

Fig. 9 Hierarchical Social and Economic Structure

becomes a hierarchy; that is, it orders itself in ranks with an élite at the top and the lesser ranks below. The élite gives leadership, those below follow. In our own society we have a long established social hierarchy. Disraeli's concept of the traditional hierarchical society remains an important element in Conservative thinking. At the head of society stands the Royal Family, the symbol of continuity, and the ancient families whose forbears were counsellors to Queen Elizabeth I, and whose descendants have contributed to Britain's government — and greatness — down to the present day. The sons of these families, brought up in the tradition that privilege implies responsibility, living with the portraits of their illustrious ancestors around them — and history, for them, is family history — educated at schools where the capacity for leadership is developed: these sons are ready to take over and manage the family estates; ready also to serve their counties and in, turn, to offer themselves for Parliament. The Salisburys, the Cecils, the Devonshires, the Churchills, the Douglas-Homes are still greatly respected in the Conservative Party and the country.

Since Disraeli's day and particularly in the early years of this century, the Conservative Party has attracted leaders from the world of commerce and industry. Businessmen like the Chamberlains of Birmingham, Bonar Law from Glasgow and Stanley Baldwin of the steel and coal firm, have shared the leadership with members of the old aristocratic families.

Similarly, the concept of 'hierarchy' has changed. We think less of an 'élite', based on hereditary title and more of 'leadership' based on ability, integrity and willingness to accept responsibility. The 'ordering in ranks' is thought of in terms of one's position in the business hierarchy, with the skilled man above the semi-skilled and unskilled and below the foreman and the manager. For, it is argued, every ordered society, every large-scale organisation, develops a hierarchical structure. An army develops one; a business enterprise (whether free enterprise or in public ownership); a profession; a church. The diagram opposite neatly, but over-simply, illustrates it. This might well be of the army, with its divisions vertically into ranks and horizontally into its specialist functions: infantry, armour, transport and supply, intelligence and so on. Or it might represent the defence services together — land, sea and air: or a large factory. It might represent society itself — a group of interrelated hierarchies, with A the business world, B the forces, C the professions, D the Church, E the political structure. At the head we might imagine the Queen as head of the State (and incidentally of the Forces and the Church) and below the various ranks according to function and responsibility.

In our own society, claim Conservatives, there is opportunity to rise. The rigid class structure of the past has gone for ever. The way up is open to ability. Conservative policy fosters this movement. The grammar schools give opportunities to the more able. They provide an atmosphere in which the 'high-fliers' can show their powers. For them the way is open — given hard work — to the university, the professions, business, politics. Thus, the élite is renewed from below.

Adequate rewards must be available at all levels, say Conservatives. Just as the skilled worker at level 5 insists on his 'differentials' to distinguish him from the unskilled at level 6 and to make it worthwhile for him to acquire and exercise skill, so each level seeks its special recompense. In such a society it is humbug, say Conservatives, for socialists to talk of 'equal shares'. They are not acceptable (not even to socialists) and if they were, they would be unjust. Equal opportunity, yes; but equal opportunity to rise — or fall — to one's just place in the hierarchy.

12.5 Free enterprise capitalism

In such a society, say Conservatives, the free-enterprise system is best. It has provided opportunities for pioneers from the merchant adventurers to the air-borne export executives of today; from the first road and rail builders to Rolls-Royce and the British Aircraft Corporation; from Henry Morris mending bicycles in an Oxford back-street to the British Motor Corporation. The founders of these great industries were men who 'backed their hunch' with hard work and their own and other people's money. They have created enterprises in which thousands of men and women with diverse abilities can find a proper place and move up as their talents warrant. Today the ambitious lorry-driver can set himself up with one lorry and soon own a fleet; the bricklayer with ability can take on a sub-contract and soon employ a team.

The nationalised industries do not foresee opportunities, will not take risks: the free-enterprise businessman can and does — witness the great, recent discoveries of oil and gas in the North Sea, very much to this nation's advantage.

Conservatives are not doctrinaire. Though they believe that free enterprise is more efficient than State monopoly, they will not denationalise an industry if convinced that it is running well. They seek to stimulate competition in industry, witness their prohibition of Resale Price Maintenance and action in taking Britain into the European Economic Community. Further, they see free enterprise and competition as a defence against tyranny. They oppose socialism because it concentrates economic and political power; capitalism diffuses it. As socialism develops there are fewer avenues of employment; ultimately there is one — and only one — employer, the State. Income is then controlled, spending done for us.

12.6 Conservative freedom

Today Conservatives put much emphasis on individual freedom; freedom for the taxpayer to spend more of his money as he likes, and have less spent for him by the State; freedom to send his children to a grammar or private school if he so wishes; freedom to spend his money on a private bed in hospital or a private doctor or dentist; freedom to buy his own house and not have to rent one from the council or a private landlord; freedom to set up in business where he can see an opening.

Is this emphasis on 'freedom' illogical in a party that stands primarily for order and discipline? No. The Conservative Party has long had its liberal element. Liberals who broke with their party over home rule for Ireland at the end of the last century and others since who could not accept socialist doctrines have joined the Conservatives. The Conservative Party, like its rival, the Labour Party, is a coalition embracing a wide range of outlook. Hence, at party conferences, when the authoritarians clamour for more rigorous policies towards criminals and the return of capital punishment, liberal Home Secretaries like Mr R. A. (now Lord) Butler or Mr Quintin Hogg (now Lord Hailsham) or Mr Robert Carr, hold the balance.

12.7 The decline of discipline

Nevertheless, traditional Conservatives today see worrying evidence of the decline of discipline and authority. Pre-marital sex, the spread of VD, too easy marriage and increasing teenage divorce are seen as the result of lax family control. Parents should exercise more authority. In schools authoritarians are fighting a rear-guard against the libertarians who have had it all their way in recent years. Children are allowed to study 'what they like'. They paint all day and cannot read or write or add up. At eighteen they have A level in art and nothing else. They are rejected by the art schools for lack of basic literacy and drift into hopelessness. Children, say Conservatives, need guidance: they must learn to do dull jobs as well as exciting ones; they must learn to accept unpleasant decisions; more should be demanded of them. Order must be established where disorder now exists. Actually the children would prefer it. If necessary, freedom to inflict corporal punishment must be restored to schools and parents.

Industry presents a similar picture of indiscipline. How is it possible for men to play cards out of sight of the foreman, for outside staff to spend an hour morning and afternoon in Fred's Caff, for work sheets to be fiddled? Clearly management is falling down on its job.

They are afraid of the unions. A man is discharged for bad time-keeping: the union insists on his reinstatement. There are irresponsible wild-cat strikes over inter-union rivalries, who shall turn the tap or bore the holes, threatened redundancies, new work schedules. The unions and their members, say Conservatives, must be forced by law to honour their contracts, otherwise anarchy in industry will grow. Crime is growing, authority must be asserted.

12.8 Tory principles

The Conservative Party, changing to meet new times (even with a grammar school product as its Parliamentary leader) but basing itself on old Tory principles: that society demands discipline; that growth and change must be slow and organic; that the nation embraces all classes and none must hold the nation to ransom; — the Conservative Party has strong support among the electorate. Since 1918, when adult suffrage was granted, Conservatives have had office for most of the time. We are, say Conservatives, a conservative nation. When the people reject conservatism, as in 1904 for the Liberals and in 1945 for Labour, they soon return to the Conservatives. After a short spell of radical reform we turn with relief to a long period of consolidation. The Labour government from 1964 to 1970 was seen in the same light. Conservatives expected the electorate to return to its traditional party and leadership at the 1970 election and were not disappointed.

Questions *for discussion and action*
1. If you are a supporter of conservatism, discuss the following criticisms of it as expounded in this chapter:
    (a) A Conservative looks to the past and not to the future.
    (b) 'Continuity' and the desire to conserve the past has led to the retention of out-dated traditions and held back necessary changes.
    (c) Freedom to 'spend as you wish' applies only to people earning £1,500 a year or more. Most workers earn less and can only afford necessities. The Conservative appeal is therefore to the middle class.
    (d) Conservatives have not really become more liberal. Freedom for the individual means freedom for the employers and the wealthy: for the workers there is still discipline and authority. In the hierarchy we must all know our places.
    (e) Men are not fundamentally competitive: mutual help on which socialism is based is stronger than competition.

(f)   Free-enterprise capitalism gives an opportunity for ten in a hundred to rise: but ninety must remain at the bottom.

2.   If you are an opponent of conservatism, discuss which you think to be the Conservatives' strongest appeal:

(a)   Its emphasis on the value of a class system which gives opportunity for and incentive to the individual to better himself.

(b)   In its call for discipline at home, school and work, and out in the streets, at football matches, etc.

(c)   In its appeal to Conservative freedom — offering the opportunity to spend your money as you wish rather than as the State demands.

3.   Get information from the Conservative Political Centre, 32 Smith Square, London, SW1, on Conservative outlook and policy and check whether or not this chapter fairly represents Conservative views. If you think it shows bias (and everyone has bias) write to the author, c/o the publisher, giving your opinion.

Chapter 13

Party attitudes: Liberal and Democratic Socialist

13.1 Consent the basis of society

The previous chapter began with Thomas Hobbes, the seventeenth-century philosopher. This begins with John Locke, who lived and wrote fifty years after Hobbes.

Locke's view of human nature differed from that of Hobbes. In *Of Civil Government*, written to justify the Revolution of 1688, he held that men had certain 'natural rights' — to life, liberty and property — and, being reasonable, recognise that other men have the same rights. However, unless there is a government to adjudicate between men, each man is a judge in his own case. This produces 'inconveniences' — not the warring anarchy that Hobbes saw, but still, unsatisfactory. It is therefore necessary to set up government, again not the authoritarian rule that Hobbes called for, but on based on the acknowledged rights of others and the freely accorded *consent* of the governed.

> ... that which begins and actually constitutes any political society is nothing but the consent of any number of freemen capable of a majority, to unite and incorporate into such a society [1].

The rule would be mild, exacting from the wrongdoer only;

> so far as calm reason and conscience dictate and what is proportional to the transgression, and which is so much as may serve for reformation and restraint.

The emphasis is on reason, moderation and consent. Government arises from men's ability to cooperate; the society established is equalitarian and libertarian.

Locke was by no means a socialist. He believed firmly in private property and one of the main aims of government, he said, was to make secure a man's possessions. Whatever a man produces by his labour is his by right, for he has embodied part of himself in it. Further, a man has a right to the land he tills because the fruits are the result of his work. A man should not gather more than he needs, nor till more than is required: for to do so would deprive others of it. On this basis there is land for everyone — if not here, then in America.

13.2 Wealth produced by labour

Locke's belief in the equality of citizens before the law and his theory that value, or wealth, is created by the labour embodied in a commodity, were taken up by socialists. If labour is the source of wealth, they asked, why is it that the labourer is poor and the landlord and capitalist rich? Clearly the labourer has been robbed, they said, and movements were set on foot to restore to the labourer 'the full-fruits of his labour'.

There was a great deal for socialists to complain about in the early years of the Industrial Revolution. Handcraftsmen had been thrown out of work by the introduction of power-driven machines. They drifted to the towns to compete with labourers driven off the land by enclosures, and by Irish immigrants. They were herded into rapidly growing but insanitary new industrial towns, without water, drains or scavenging. They worked long hours in unhealthy conditions at low wages. When they asked for increased wages they were told that wages could never rise for any length of time above subsistence level. Wages, they were told, would be just sufficient for a worker to feed himself and bring up enough children to satisfy the demand for labour. If wages rose higher, then labourers would produce more children and competition among them would drive wages down to their former level. This was 'the iron law of wages'.

The economists who preached this hopeless doctrine to 'the labouring classes' justified the payment of rent to landowners and profits to industrialists on the ground that there were three 'agents of production'; not merely 'labour', but also land and capital, and the owners of land and capital were entitled to their share of the product.

13.3 Marx and class–war

Socialists refused to accept these views which destined workers to unending misery. Karl Marx, a political exile from Germany, who made a deep study of British conditions, drew together much earlier socialist thought and gave it a solid theoretical basis. There were two classes, he said, the capitalists, who owned the land and the factories, and the 'proletariat' (the working people) with only their labour to sell. Capitalists, owning 'the means of production', kept wages at subsistence level. They retained a permanent 'reserve army' of unemployed, so that there were always men ready to step into the job of a man who pressed for higher wages. Goods were sold well above the cost of production: the excess was the owners' profit. This surplus really belonged to the workers whose labour had created the value. There was, said Marx, a continual war between the workers and their employers as the former struggled to increase their wages and were beaten down by the employers greedy for profit. To the argument that profits were the reward of the capitalists' thrift and abstinence, in saving to invest in factories and machines, socialists replied that these also were the product of labour — they were 'crystallised' labour — of which the workers had earlier been robbed.

Socialists, said Marx, should make the workers realise that the real cause of their troubles was the capitalist system of production and its attendant class-war. As capitalists competed with each other and the rate of profit fell, that war would be intensified. Independent craftsmen and small producers would be squeezed out and sink into the ranks of the proletariat. There would be increasing misery. The task of the workers and their unions was to fight, not just for a bigger share of the product, but to take over the mines and the factories — to 'expropriate the expropriators'.

In the latter half of the nineteenth century these doctrines were advocated by a growing number of working-class socialists and their middle-class allies. They worked within the trade unions: they urged that every adult should have a vote; they sought the establishment of a 'Labour' party to represent the working class, independent of the Liberal and Tory parties, who, at that time, won working-class votes by promising social reforms and legislation to improve factory conditions and the regulation of trade unions.

In times of good trade, improved living standards were secured by the unions and the appeal of the socialists for a transformation of society went unheeded. In times of bad trade socialist ideas made headway.

13.4 The Independent Labour Party and the Fabian Society

Not all socialists were class-war Marxist. Keir Hardie, a Scottish miner, probably the most influential figure in the British socialist movement from the 1880s to his death in 1915, opposed the doctrine of the class-war. Agreeing that there was a conflict of interest between the owners of property and those who work for wages, he held that it was the object of socialism to remove the causes which produced this antagonism. 'Socialism', he said, 'makes war upon a system, not a class.' He formed, and led, the Independent Labour Party (the ILP) which carried the bulk of socialist propaganda until the 1930s. It was a 'movement' rather than a party. Its aim was the establishment of a democratic socialist commonwealth, concerned not only with economic standards but with the quality of human life. Its members preached socialism at the street corners with religious fervour. Many of them drew their inspiration from Christian upbringings, lacing their speeches with Biblical texts. They condemned a system where so many were compelled to live on 'the crumbs that fell from the rich man's table'. Their appeals for solidarity were based on the brotherhood of man (stemming from the fatherhood of God) rather than on the class-war.

The Fabian Society, a group of middle-class intellectuals, undertook research into social problems with the aim of influencing, by permeation, existing political parties. It urged the gradual transformation of society by the adoption of 'gas & water' socialism; that is, the extension of municipal and State ownership of public utility services.

Throughout the early years of the twentieth century socialism was advocated by such writers as H. G. Wells and Bernard Shaw; later by H. N. Brailsford, G. D. H. Cole, H. J. Laski and others.

There would be no hope of any substantial improvement in the lives of working people, they said (echoing Marx, but using a more persuasive language) until industry was taken out of the hands of private capitalists and put under social ownership. Then industry would be organised for service, not to extract the largest profit for the owner. There would be 'production for use, not profit'. Profits retained and ploughed back for improved equipment would belong to us all. Industry would be planned and no longer subject to the boom and slump inevitable under unplanned, competitive capitalism. The worker would be a partner in the nationalised industries and 'workers' control' progressively extended. The land would be nationalised and put to its most valuable social use. Houses for people would come before luxury flats and hotels. Landlords would no longer be able to cream off the continually rising value of land in towns and cities. Every increase in its value would go back to the people who had created it: those who live and work there. Further, the provision of education and medicine, the support of people in sickness, unemployment and similar misfortunes, provision of opportunities for recreation and enjoyment of the arts would be the responsibility of the State. Thus, with society concerned for the well-being of *all* its members, individual competitiveness would give way to mutual aid: men would at last feel themselves 'members one of another'. Capitalism, with its jungle law, would be replaced by socialism where 'wealth which common effort creates is a pool which belongs to all' [2]. Each would contribute according to his ability and draw out according to need. Strict equality of income was not the aim. As R. H. Tawney said in his classic work *Equality* [3] the first claim on society was a reasonable provision for everyone. When that had been achieved no one objected to exceptional rewards for exceptional responsibility.

Tawney attacked the Conservative view that 'equality of opportunity' was needed so that a few might rise above their fellows.

'The day when a thousand donkeys could be induced to sweat by the prospect of a carrot that could be eaten by one' was long over (p. 123). Equality of opportunity.

> is right in insisting on the necessity of opening a free career to aspiring talent; it is wrong in suggesting that opportunities to rise, which can, of their very nature, be seized only by the very few, are a substitute for a general diffusion of the means of civilisation, which are needed by all men, whether they rise or not and which those who cannot climb the economic ladder, and who sometimes indeed, do not desire to climb it, may turn to as good account as those who can (p. 120).

Violent contrasts of wealth, arising mainly from inheritance, were an affront and must be dealt with.

The need is to liberate in all men, not the few, the powers that 'make for energy and refinement', in the faith that 'the differences between men are less important and fundamental than their common humanity' (p. 84).

13.5 The politics of socialism

How was this socialism to be achieved? By Parliamentary means, said socialists at the end of the nineteenth century. First there must be a separate 'Labour Party', based on the trade unions, and secondly, it must have a socialist aim.

The party was established in 1900, mainly with trade union support, but made little progress. In 1918, with the restoration of peace after the First World War, the Labour Party emerged as a definitely socialist party.

During the war, many industries had been taken over and run by the State. People who had been told before the war that increased expenditure on social services would ruin the country, found that £8 million a day could be spent for war purposes without apparent ruin. It was only during the war that everyone was able to find work. The Labour Party, in its new 1918 constitution therefore promised

> to secure to the producers by hand and brain, the full fruits of their industry and the most equitable distribution thereof that may be possible, upon the basis of the common ownership of the means of production and the best obtainable system of popular administration and control of each industry and service.

Its detailed programme called for the nationalisation of the railways, coal-mines and production of electrical power. The profits from these industries and steeply graduated taxes on incomes and riches were to be used for economic improvement and for the maintenance of the aged, sick and infirm. This programme, moderate and reasonable as it may seem today, made little appeal in competition with the policies of the war-time coalition parties fighting together under the leadership of Lloyd George — 'the man who won the war' — who cashed in on the war-time hysteria promised to 'Hang the Kaiser' and 'squeeze Germany until the pips squeak', promising also 'homes fit for heroes to live in' and better social conditions. Labour won more seats than before, but lost some of its better known leaders.

After a brief post-war boom in which living standards rose, there was an attack on wages which were reduced faster than prices, so that by 1921 the wage earners' standard of living was *below* the pre-1914 level, itself miserable, and remained so until 1926 [4]. Was this what the 'war for democracy' had been fought for, asked the socialists? Is this the best that capitalism can do? Socialists drove home the reality of 'poverty amidst potential plenty', quoting social surveys made in the 1920s of Merseyside, Sheffield, Bristol and Southampton (not by any means the worst areas in the country), which showed that these towns had from 12–15 per cent of families and from 22–30 per cent of their children living below the poverty line [5].

Sir John Boyd Orr in *Food, Health and Income* (Macmillan, 1936) showed that one-tenth of the nation's population, including one-quarter of its children, were able to spend only 4s 0d per head weekly on food and had a diet lacking *all* the constituents most necessary to health. At this very time, socialists pointed out, there were people in this country with vast wealth. Indeed, a mere 2.5 per cent of the population owned nearly two-thirds of its wealth: the remaining 97 per cent shared the rest [6].

But the greatest criticism arose over unemployment. By 1923 there were over 11 per cent of insured workers without work; by 1930, nearly 20 per cent. This was spread very unevenly throughout the country; it was worst in areas where Britain's basic industries were situated — in Wales, Scotland and the North, where nearly 30 per cent of the people were without work. This showed, said socialists, that

Poverty and unemployment in the inter-war years

capitalism had failed: it could not deal with the basic industries — coal, iron, shipbuilding, textiles — on which the nation's wealth had been built.

In the early 1920s the Labour Party, pressing the case for a socialist alternative to capitalism, and promising to 'cure unemployment' grew rapidly, outpaced the Liberal Party, which declined through internal dissension. Labour formed brief minority governments in 1924 and 1929. In the latter year it was the largest single party in the House of Commons for the first time. In these minority governments, Labour, whether it wished to or not, could not introduce 'socialism' that would be unacceptable to the Liberals without whom it had no majority in the House. But it was, itself, uncertain about what it should do. 'Socialism' at this stage was still largely a propaganda term. No one had worked out in detail how it should be applied.

In 1931 there was a world economic crisis with 3 million unemployed in Great Britain, 6 million in Germany and 15 million in the USA. Banks failed in Austria and Germany, Wall Street (the financial centre in New York) panicked and there was a run on our gold reserves. The Labour government, which, like its Conservative predecessors had failed to cure unemployment, split on the economies called for by the bankers, especially cuts in the already inadequate unemployment allowance. The government fell and was succeeded by a National government, a coalition of Conservative, Liberal and a handful of

Labour Members. At the ensuing general election Labour was routed.

When war broke out in 1939 Mr Chamberlain's Conservative government was soon replaced by a coalition under Mr Churchill, in which Labour took an important second place. Party differences were set aside as the nation concentrated on winning the war. After victory in Europe the coalition was dissolved and the election (unlike that of 1919) was fought on party lines. The electorate associated the Conservatives with long inter-war years of unemployment and poverty; Labour with the prospect of better times ahead.

13.6 Labour's post-war victory in 1945

In 1945 Labour swept in, had a majority for the first time in its history, and introduced a socialist programme. It nationalised the Bank of England, the mines, railways, road and air transport and gas and electricity generation and supply. This was substantially the socialist policy of 1918 brought up to date. It extended the social services and introduced a National Health Service on lines agreed by the war-time coalition, and rapidly expanded the building industry to provide houses, four-fifths of which were for working-class occupation. It maintained full employment. Late in the Parliament it nationalised steel in the teeth of Conservative opposition. It gave freedom to 400 million citizens in India and Pakistan, formerly under British rule and started the peoples of the Commonwealth on the road to independence.

According to many, this was the high watermark of socialist achievement. The Conservatives gained control in the general election of 1951 and held power until 1964.

By the time Labour came back, its outlook had been substantially changed. Conservative thinking also had changed. Labour was putting less emphasis on the nationalisation of industry and Conservatives, accepting a large measure of public ownership, were interfering more and more in the economic life of the country. Electors found this similarity of behaviour puzzling. Did it mean that the Conservatives had become socialists and the Labour Party now supported capitalism: modified, no doubt, but still in essence capitalism?

Not quite. Although party attitudes had changed substantially there were still fundamental differences between them as will be seen in later chapters.

The change had been brought about by the adoption by both parties of policies designed to end the scourge of mass-unemployment. They were the work of Mr J. M. (later Lord) Keynes, a Liberal economist who had changed the economic and political thinking of many people and the action of the main political parties on this hitherto intractable social problem. The revolution that Keynes created, bringing with it a radical change in the balance of political and economic forces within the nation, is described in detail in the next chapter.

Meanwhile, here are questions on this chapter.

Questions *for discussion and action*

1. Consider the following criticisms of socialism as expounded in this chapter:

    (a) Socialists preach the class-war which divides the nation, whereas Conservatives want 'one-nation'.

    (b) Socialists talk of equality but in practice every section of the working class fights for its 'differentials'.

    (c) Socialist demands for equality are based on envy. Conservatives recognise that there are differences between people and that the higher the contribution of skill and responsibility the higher should be the reward. They are against punitive taxation on higher incomes.

    (d) The private enterprise system, where the workers at all levels have an incentive to greater effort, is more efficient than a bureaucratically run system of nationalised industries, which, despite charging high prices, still make losses.

    (e) Socialist governments, by taking economic as well as political power, are moving towards totalitarianism under which the State will decide our incomes and how we are to spend them and otherwise regiment our lives, as in the Soviet Union. The claim that Socialists are libertarian and Conservatives authoritarian is therefore false: it reverses the truth.

2. Many workers, including coal-miners and railwaymen, who worked for the nationalisation of their industries, were disappointed at the results. Why should this have been so? Examine the case for 'participation' by the workers in the making of decisions that affect them and it. What is meant by 'workers' control' of industry? Find out what you can about workers' partnership in industry (e.g. The John Lewis Partnership, The Scott Bader Company, The Zeiss Company of Switzerland). Examine the Liberal Party's proposals for co-ownership.

3. Bernard Shaw advocated equality of incomes. He condemned the system of 'to each what he can grab'. Is that the system in Great Britain today? What attempts have been made to introduce a fairer system? Are these necessarily 'equalitarian'?

4. At present nearly every section of the population is concerned to maintain its income 'differentials'. Assuming that you are a believer in greater equality of incomes, how would you persuade people to train to take on additional responsibilities, to 'do the

dirty work'? (Shaw suggested shorter hours for the latter.)

5. 'What is economically just may not be politically possible.' This statement is used to counter arguments for a redistribution of the national income and to urge that changes can only be brought about by allocating the extra wealth produced each year to varying purposes (e.g. so much to increased wages, so much to pensioners, so much to education and so on). Consider the extent to which the government redistributes our incomes at present. Could (and should) more be done — or less? What, in your opinion, are the most urgent claims on increases in the national income?

6. 'Anyone who does less than her share of work and takes her full share of the wealth is a thief.' (Shaw) [7]. 'If any would not work, neither should he eat.' (St Paul.) It is a socialist principle that every able bodied person should do his or her share of the necessary work.

Consider the following happenings that enable people to live without working:

(a) Inheritance of wealth;
(b) Winning the pools;
(c) Winning the large prizes on Premium Bonds;
(d) Dropping out.

What would you do in respect of each of these happenings to ensure that everyone did his share of the work essential for the production of the food, clothes, etc., which we all need?

7. Get information from the Labour Party, Transport House, Smith Square, London SW1, on socialist outlook and policy and check whether or not this chapter fairly represents Labour views. If you think it shows bias (and everyone has bias) write to the author, c/o the publisher, giving your opinion.

Chapter 14

The Keynesian revolution

14.1 The problem of unemployment

In the inter-war years the key question was unemployment. People in all parties were worried. It was a shocking thing that there were un-employed mineworkers when people lacked coal, that textile workers were out of work when people lacked clothes: that skilled building workers were unable to build the houses that slum-dwellers and over-crowded families needed. And there was the misery of the unemployed man himself, rejected by society, willing but unable to find work.

No party knew how to tackle the problem. The two brief Labour governments of the inter-war years were as ineffective as the Conservative.

Then, a government faced with slackening trade, increasing unemployment, less income from taxation and more required for unemployment relief, did what any individual person would do in hard times: it tightened its belt and cut its spending. In fact this made things worse, for, with less money being spent, still more people were thrown out of work and the slump deepened. In the early 1930s between 2 and 3 million people were unemployed, some 12—20 per cent of the employed population.

14.2 The new thinking of J. M. Keynes

In 1936 an economist and former civil servant, J. M. (later Lord) Keynes published his *General Theory of Employment, Interest and*

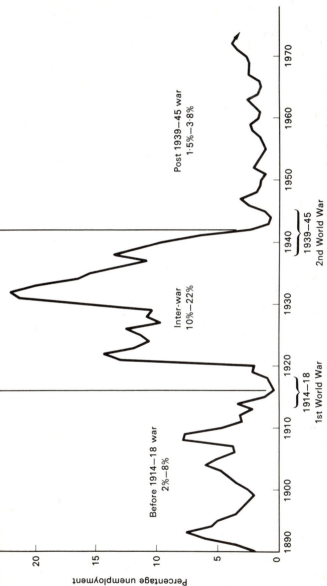

Mass unemployment—the scourge of inter-war politics—has been conquered: but new problems of inflation and balance of payments difficulties have arisen

Source: Employment policy (CMD6527 HMSO) for 1890—1900 The British Economy; Key Statistics 1900—1970 London and Cambridge Economic Services and *The Times*

Fig. 10 Unemployment in the United Kingdom 1890—1972 as a percentage of employed population

Money [1], which revolutionised thinking — and in time, action — on the way to avoid mass unemployment.

Keynes noted that what we spend, individually, someone else will earn. Further, that the total that we spend — taking us all together — is the total that we, again taking us all together, will earn. Now most of us spend all our incomes, especially if we are among the lower paid. But some save. If, in any year, we put that saving in a sock or under the bed and spend less, then the total of other people's incomes will be that much less: and as nothing has happened to change the level of individual incomes, it means that fewer people will be employed. But if we 'invest' the savings, that is find some businessman who will spend it on installing new machinery or on raw materials or wages, then total spending (and employment) will go back to its former level. The same will occur if the savings are put in a bank or insurance company and these organisations lend it out for someone to spend.

It was noted that business went in cycles: there were periods of confidence, when businessmen borrowed from the public and the banks and increased their spending on new factories and equipment. More people were employed, they in turn had more to spend and so the economy expanded. At a later date businessmen became fearful about the future: they stopped building new factories and re-equipping them: the companies making machines and heavy equipment would be slack. Men would be stood off, have less to spend, and, generally, industry would contract. Keynes noted, however, that the economy, even when doing well, settled at a position well short of full employment. Unemployment never fell below 10 per cent in the inter-war years. He concluded that unless someone did something about it, the economy would continue to fluctuate and usually about a point where there was still a substantial number of unemployed. Now, who should 'do' that something? Clearly, said Keynes: the government. It should ensure that total demand (or spending) is sufficient to create 'a high and stable level of employment'. To achieve this, the government, in times of high unemployment must pump money into the economy: that is, must spend more than it raises in taxes, and must do so until the extra spending it initiates has spread through the economy, production has picked up and everyone — or nearly everyone — is at work. Incomes would increase by more than the amount of the government's initial spending, because the money would be spent and re-spent, producing a 'multiplier' effect. Thus not all the extra spending required would need to come from the government. As the economy expanded businessmen would spend more on new equipment and borrow more from investors and the banks. As unemployment fell it would be easier for unions to get higher wages.

The government's job was to ensure that these increases in

spending were sufficient, in total, to take the economy to the point of full employment.

It must not be assumed that unemployment can fall to nil. There are always some people changing jobs; some industries grow and some decline; people's tastes change, new inventions suggest new wants: machines take the place of men. Allowing for all these factors Sir William Beveridge, the economist, thought that about the best we could do would be to reduce unemployment to a minimum of 3 per cent [2]. (Actually, in post-war years, it has ranged between 1½ and 3½ per cent.)

Keynes's theory called for radically different behaviour from that of pre-Keynesian times. Previously, as noted, when unemployment was high, governments and businessmen cut down their spending. To do otherwise seemed madness. Now they were urged to do the opposite. Further, governments were asked to 'budget for a deficit', i.e., spend more than they raised in taxes, borrowing the difference which, by former standards was the height of imprudence. It meant that the 'National Debt', that is the government's accumulated borrowings, would rise.

It was some time before Keynes's revolutionary views were acted upon. In the USA President Roosevelt experimented cautiously. He worked originally on the 'pump-priming' theory, thinking that, as a pump will start up only after water has been poured in at the top, if the government spent large sums in excess of tax revenue, it would give the economy a boost and that as business improved businessmen would increase investment and progress would be maintained. Although demand increased by three or four times the amount injected by the government (in accordance with Keynes's multiplier theory) as soon as the government's 'deficit financing' was reduced, so demand fell away. Keynes rejected 'pump priming' and urged persistent spending in excess of taxation to keep the economy at a high level of activity. In 1937 the US government, in response to criticism (from pre-Keynesian thinkers) that a succession of budget deficits was increasing the National Debt to alarming levels, severely curtailed its spending. The effect was the sharpest decline in economic activity that the United States had experienced. 'The most shocking aspect of the 1937 recession', wrote Dudley Dillard the American economist, 'was that it occurred when there were approximately 8 million men still out of work [3]'.

Experiments of this kind were not tried in the United Kingdom. There was a gradual improvement in business activity in the later 1930s but it was not until the vast rearmament programmes here and in the United States got under way on the outbreak of war in 1939 that unemployment vanished — and the arguments of J. M. Keynes went home.

14.3 The Second World War, 1939-45

Keynes resumed his work at the British Treasury on the outbreak of the Second World War. Hitherto the problem had been insufficient demand. Now, with everyone in the forces or at work, incomes were higher. The government was pouring almost unlimited sums into the production of armaments. But although incomes were high, the flow of goods and services *for consumers* was reduced: thus the pre-war situation was reversed. Keynes saw that the great need was to reduce consumer spending, otherwise prices would rise sharply. He recommended:

- (i) Increased taxation — though there is a limit to what is politically possible even in wartime.
- (ii) Increased saving — through persuasive propaganda to 'save for victory'. And
- (iii) Compulsory saving — a new idea, this, to be achieved by an additional 'tax', to be refunded after the war in the form of post-war credits.

Keynes's view was that without a substantial element of compulsory saving the extra purchasing power available would drive up prices — people would in fact get no more consumer goods than were being produced but would merely pay more for them. Compulsory savings would deprive them of no real benefit but would provide a nest egg for the future. At the end of the war the less well-off would have a share of National Savings as well as the better-off. Besides, it would provide a reserve of purchasing power to release into the economy should a post-war slump threaten. The idea of compulsory savings was adopted, although not to the extent that Keynes advocated: retail prices rose much less in the Second World War than in the First, a tribute to Keynes's influence. It was with this experience that we approached the post-war era.

14.4 Post-war plans for full employment

In May 1944 the war-time coalition government turned its mind to post-war reconstruction and issued a White Paper (Cmd. 6527) on 'Employment Policy'.

'The Government accept,' it said, 'as one of their primary aims and responsibilities, the maintenance of a high and stable level of employment after the war,' adding the sound Keynesian doctrine that, 'A country will not suffer from mass unemployment so long as the total demand for its goods and services is maintained at a high level.'

Britain had two special problems: one flowed from the decline of certain basic industries which left whole areas with severe unemployment even when the rest of the country was prosperous. To these areas the government must persuade, or direct, new industries, while helping workers who wished to do so to move elsewhere. The second problem was Britain's dependence on overseas trade. Imports of raw materials are necessary if our factories are to keep working; and we must import some half of our food if we are to maintain a population of 55 million in these small islands. These essential imports must be paid for by exports. Our industries must be competitive, therefore, in world markets and world markets themselves must be prosperous. 'The Government,' said the White Paper, 'are therefore seeking to create, through collaboration between the nations, conditions of international trade which will make it possible for all countries to pursue policies of full-employment to their mutual advantage.'

14.5 The post-war years

What has been Britain's experience since the war? Both Labour and Conservative governments have applied Keynesian policies and unemployment has averaged a mere 1½ per cent, ranging from 1.2 per cent to just over 3 per cent. Effectively, then, we have had 'full employment'. But this achievement has brought with it new problems. For in many of the post-war years our difficulty has been excessive demand (as in the war) not lack of demand.

Why has this happened?

In broad terms, government spending (especially when undertaken from borrowing rather than taxation, i.e. from deficit financing; see p.129), added to businessmen's spending on new equipment and our own spending from incomes at a high level on account of full employment, have, from time to time, outrun production. If total spending is increased beyond the point when everyone is in work and all machines are fully utilised, it can result only in rising prices, difficulty in keeping up our exports and the drawing in of imports because of unsatisfied demand. Thus, whenever unemployment has been at a low level, we have experienced a 'balance of payments deficit'. Imports have exceeded exports and to pay for the excess we have drawn on our gold and dollar reserves. To 'protect the reserves', post-war governments have 'deflated', that is, taken steps to reduce spending: by increasing taxation, restricting hire-purchase, putting up the rate of interest and making borrowing of all types more difficult. This has led to a reduction of imports, greater exports and a surplus on balance of payments: but at the same time a considerable increase in unemployment. Then, if unemployment rose above, say, 2 or 2½ per cent, the government would reverse the process – stimulate spending – and unemployment would fall: but be followed by balance of payments difficulties and the whole process would be repeated. The diagram opposite illustrates the point.

Of course, the problem is not as simple as that described here: on certain occasions special factors have been at work. Sometimes the excessive spending was the result of unusual amounts of business investment – good in itself but, taken with other items, contributing to our difficulties. Sometimes the prices of imports rose because wars in Korea or Vietnam led to an increase in world demand for strategic materials. And the remedial action taken by governments varied according to their view of the situation.

When the Labour government took over in 1945 the war had so impoverished us that we were unable to pay for our necessary imports. During the war we had been supplied by the USA under 'Lease-lend', which deferred payment until the war was over. Lease-lend ceased the day the war in Europe ended. To tide us over the early post-war years the USA made a loan on generous terms and wiped off all Lease-lend debts. Stupendous efforts were made by us to increase our exports and by 1948 we achieved a small surplus. However, a condition of the US loan was that we removed exchange controls, and this premature action led to a loss of gold and dollars and forced us to devalue the pound in 1949. This action made our exports cheaper and imports dearer, so that we could look forward to a surplus balance of payments. But it also raised prices at home and at the general election in 1950 the Labour government, which had been much criticised for slowness in ending war-time rationing and controls, for its appeals for 'wage-restraint' and acceptance of austerity, had its majority cut to eight. Devaluation produced a substantial surplus on balance of payments in 1950, but the outbreak of war in Korea in June 1950 turned the cost of imports against us and we went into substantial deficit in 1951.

To meet the cost of the war and to deal with the balance of payments deficit, the Labour government raised income tax from 9s 0d to 9s 6d in the £ and doubled purchase tax on cars, radios, refrigerators, etc. At the general election of October 1951, Labour lost and the Conservatives were in with a majority of seventeen. The severe deflationary measures of the outgoing government increased unemployment, which went higher than anticipated because of the loss of export markets, notably for cotton. But substantial surpluses on the balance of payments for the next three years enabled the Conservative government to put the austerity measures into reverse. Income tax was reduced, demand expanded and unemployment fell steadily until, by 1955, it was again at the low level of 1.2 per cent. There were two special factors at this time: capital expenditure by businessmen was growing at

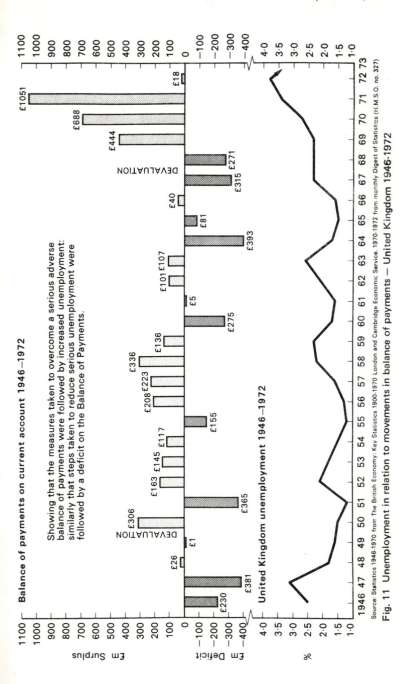

Balance of payments on current account 1946—1972

Showing that the measures taken to overcome a serious adverse balance of payments were followed by increased unemployment: similarly that steps taken to reduce serious unemployment were followed by a deficit on the Balance of Payments.

£m Surplus

DEVALUATION

£306

£163 £145 £117

£155

£208 £223

£336

£136

£5

£275

£101 £107

£393

£81

£40

£315

£271

DEVALUATION

£444

£688

£1051

£18

£m Deficit

£26

£1

£381

£230

£365

United Kingdom unemployment 1946—1972

%

Source: Statistics 1946-1970 from The British Economy: Key Statistics 1900-1970 London and Cambridge Economic Service. 1970-1972 from monthly Digest of Statistics (H.M.S.O. no. 327)

Fig. 11 Unemployment in relation to movements in balance of payments — United Kingdom 1946-1972

1946 47 48 49 50 51 52 53 54 55 56 57 58 59 60 61 62 63 64 65 66 67 68 69 70 71 72 73

about 15 per cent a year and in the pre-election Budget of 1955 the standard rate of income tax was again reduced. At the general election of 1955 the Conservative position was consolidated but, by the end of the year, the inevitable deficit on balance of payments appeared.

In 1957 and 1958 demand was cut back by the Chancellor, Mr Thorneycroft. Bank rate was raised and hire-purchase regulations stiffened. The balance of payments went back into surplus for four years — the best post-war showing — but unemployment rose steadily, reaching 2.6 per cent in 1959. This level was considered excessive, and measures to produce expansion were again introduced: Bank rate was brought down, hire-purchase eased; income and purchase tax reduced (it was election year again) and unemployment fell. And, once more, as business boomed, and unemployment got down to 1.6 per cent, the balance of payments went into deficit for two years, 1960 and 1961.

Rather tardily the government took action: in July 1961, the medicine was administered, as before; demand was cut back by increased bank rate, increases in indirect taxes and cuts in government spending. There were this time only two years of surplus on balance of payments; and unemployment went over 3 per cent. The government, to tackle this, the highest level of unemployment since the war, early in 1963 set about increasing demand. Retirement pensions and national insurance benefits were raised, income tax and purchase tax reduced. Unemployment fell steeply to a more normal figure of 1½ per cent. There was a general election in 1964 and the Labour Party won only to find that it had inherited a record balance of payments deficit. It had fought on a programme very different from that of 1945 and it is necessary to pause in this survey to examine it.

14.6 The effect of Keynesianism on party policies

Labour had won its 1945 victory on the traditional socialist case. The Labour government nationalised the basic industries and introduced the social measures planned by the war-time coalition. However, the expected benefits of nationalisation were not apparent. Profits that were to flow into the public exchequer did not appear: indeed, there were mounting deficits. Coal-mining and the railways had been in serious difficulties before nationalisation: compensation had been paid for them and interest had to be paid on compensation stock whether they were profitable or otherwise. Further, the mines and railways needed vast sums of capital expenditure to bring them up to date, after years of neglect and war-time use. Electricity production needed exceptional expansion. Prices, too, had been held down in the public sector, by political pressures — but this was less obvious to the citizen, to whom all prices without distinction seemed to rise. Under these pressures, the Labour Party's case for nationalisation changed: it was less to secure profits said party spokesmen, than to improve the efficiency of these industries; to end generations of industrial strife (as in the mines); to provide a service, even when not profitable, as on country rail and road transport routes. There was an even more important reason: the national control of these industries, said socialists, enabled spending on new equipment (power stations, electrification, automation) to be planned ahead and this contributed considerably to the steady expansion of the 'capital goods industries' whose fluctuations in pre-war days had been the cause of much unemployment. They were one of the instruments of control needed by the government to maintain total demand at a high level, on Keynesian lines, and ensure full employment. The changed attitude to nationalisation was apparent when, at the end of its period of office, the Labour government nationalised the steel industry. Steel was a profitable industry. Then why take it over? asked the Conservatives, for if it made profits it must be efficient; it had organised itself into large units and set up a board to ensure that it did not act against the public interest. Socialists replied that the future of an industry on which so much of the economy depended could not be left to irresponsible private decisions. Under its near monopoly organisation it might seek to produce less steel — at a higher profit — than the nation's industry needed. Why, for example, were we importing so much steel? The argument was now about power: a democratic society must determine its economic, as well as its political, future.

Steel was nationalised by Labour in 1951 and denationalised following the Conservative victory in that year. Conservatives held power for the thirteen years from 1951 to 1964.

In opposition, the Labour Party had time to think out its position. When Hugh Gaitskell succeeded to the leadership on Mr Attlee's retirement in 1955 he sought to give the party a new 'image'. He proposed to change the party's constitution, clause 4 of which called for the nationalisation of the 'means of production, distribution and exchange'. Gaitskell thought that, in view of the widespread disillusionment with nationalisation, an amendment limiting nationalisation to industries 'failing the nation', instancing some examples of that failure and outlining methods other than nationalisation for bringing industries under social control, would make a more realistic appeal than the wholesale nationalisation of clause 4. However, there was a rallying of the Left wing of the party in defence of the traditional wording and after some acrimonious discussion the matter was dropped. Gaitskell's view was that nationalisation was a means, and not the only means, to the desired end — socialism — and 'socialism was about equality'. The first claim on society was a reasonable provision for everyone. There would be a new advance towards educational equality and improvement in the social services. Labour would make a wider use of resources to end 'public squalor', if necessary at the expense of 'private affluence'. Violent contrasts of wealth were an affront and must be dealt with.

This policy, it was thought, was not only a right one, but would appeal to a wider section of the electorate than that which had hitherto supported Labour.

On the unexpected death of Hugh Gaitskell in 1963 Harold Wilson was elected to the leadership of the Labour Party. He developed Gaitskell's argument. The need, he said, was to ensure a dynamic economy in both the public and private sectors so that, year by year, the increase in wealth could be used for the civilised ends of which Gaitskell (and Tawney before him) had spoken. There would be 'a mobilisation of all our resources of energy, manpower, brains, imagination and skill'.

By planned expansion we would break out from the 'stop—go' cycle which had held down Britain's economic growth to an average rate below that of other European countries. There would be a 'breakthrough, to an exciting and wonderful period in our history' [4].

Housing, education and health would have top priority: avoidable poverty that still existed in our so-called affluent society would be tackled; the land speculator, take-over bidder and tax evader would be put in second place to 'the useful people on whom the welfare and well-being of the nation depend' [5].

The new policy was criticised by Left-wing socialists as an attempt to 'make capitalism work' and that was best left to Conservatives. In fact it appealed to the electorate. In 1964 and 1966 the Labour Party secured a majority and put this policy into operation.

But Conservative policies also had changed under the impact of Keynesian ideas. Who in the 1930s would have believed that Conservatives would adopt the Keynesian thesis set out in the 1944 White Paper on Full Employment (see p. 130)? True, a few Conservatives like Harold Macmillan had urged these policies in the 1930s but had been very near expulsion from their party for doing so. Post-war Conservative governments acted, as we have seen, to control the economy by the use of taxation and financial controls to avoid the extremes of excessive unemployment on the one hand and balance of payments difficulties on the other. They introduced measures to induce industries to move to the depressed areas where unemployment was high and persistent. Except for the steel industry and part of road transport they did not denationalise industries taken over by the Labour government. They advocated a voluntary wages policy. Under Mr Macmillan, as Prime Minister, in March 1962 they set up the National Economic Development Council (Neddie) to stimulate the growth of the economy: a first essay in 'indicative planning', that is, a statement of possible objectives for the public and private sectors of industry which representatives of employers and the trade unions were asked to accept and work for. This had its critics in the Conservative Party who asked what was happening to the party of private enterprise which had consistently opposed state planning and the interference by governments in business affairs. This was socialism and best left to the socialists.

At this point we must return to our survey of the economic action taken by governments of both the main parties under the influence of Keynesian ideas. The experience of the Labour governments of 1964—70 and the reaction of the Conservative government of 1970 to it are taken up in the next chapter.

Chapter 15

Policy and action since the mid-'sixties

15.1 Labour and the economic problem 1964-70

To what extent was Mr Wilson's Labour government able to 'break out' from 'stop—go' and ensure steady expansion through planning, a rise in the standard of living and the revitalisation of the social services?

The balance of payments crisis inherited by the Labour government was worse than most people had expected. The deficit on current trading was £350 million to which must be added net long-term investment overseas of £400 million. This £400 million and much of the long-term investment overseas of the previous four years had been financed from short-term borrowing from abroad. This left Britain in a vulnerable position. When the extent of our deficit was published many people abroad who had lent us money on short term, fearing that the £ would be devalued, called in their loans. Additionally some speculators at home and abroad, hoping to profit from devaluation, sold sterling heavily so as to force devaluation.

To meet this 'flight from the £' the Labour government took traditional action: The Bank of England was instructed to borrow from the International Monetary Fund and overseas Central Banks to pay off our pressing short-term creditors. At home, bank rate was raised, credit restricted, an extra tax put on imports and restrictions imposed on long-term overseas lending. Although this was the 'stop' element of 'stop—go' that the Labour Party had criticised when in opposition, it was not particularly held against the government as its increased majority in the 1966 general election showed. The measures were no doubt thought to be unavoidable and the electorate was impressed by the energy with which the problems were being tackled.

A Department of Economic Affairs had been set up with the dynamic Mr George Brown as its first Minister. Its Economic Plan set targets for increased production year by year until 1970. Much of the increased production was to go into exports 'to get our balance of payments right'. Some was to go into re-equipping our industries, some to improved social services, some to increased spending by all of us.

An essential part of the Economic Plan was a 'prices and incomes policy'. Over the previous ten years, while output had increased by an average of 3 per cent a year, wages and salaries had risen by 6½ per cent and profits by 6 per cent. The inevitable result of this was that prices had risen by 3 per cent a year. (It was the same process as we noted earlier in considering Keynes's war-time proposals (p. 130).) Inflation at this rate was bad: rising prices made exporting more difficult and at home pensioners and people on low incomes suffered a declining standard. And it did the people with rising incomes no good: they could only buy the goods that had been produced so that their real incomes rose by only 3 per cent. It drew in imports from abroad, but sooner or later these had to be paid for. What was needed, then, the Plan explained, was that 'money incomes should keep in line with real output'. This would ensure 'price stability and the orderly growth of incomes'.

The policy for incomes, then, required that, as production was expected to increase at 3½ per cent a year until 1970, wages, salaries and other incomes should, by voluntary agreement, not be raised by more than 3–3½ per cent a year throughout that period. Exception was made for lower-paid workers, workers with good productivity records and workers in industries where there was a shortage of labour: these were entitled to slightly more. A National Board for Incomes and Prices was set up to act as a watch-dog.

The deflationary 'stop' policy worked. Exports increased substantially in 1965 and the balance of payments deficit was reduced to £80 million. The voluntary Prices and Incomes policy was not so successful. Everyone felt entitled to the 'norm' of 3–3½ per cent and others fitted themselves into the exceptions entitled to more. The result was that, between the fourth quarter of 1964 and the first half of 1966, *output* per hour in manufacturing rose by 3¾ per cent but hourly *earnings* rose by 10 per cent. The difference was taken out in increased prices [1].

In July 1966 there was another run on our gold and dollar reserves. To convince overseas bankers, who were again called in for aid, an incomes 'freeze' was initiated as well as the usual restrictionist 'stop' measures. The 'Freeze' was unprecedented. It covered everyone and it was compulsory. It was to last six months, from July to December 1966, and to be followed by a period of 'severe restraint'. Legislation was passed, to be used only as a last resort against trade unions and others who would not conform. The run on the £ was stemmed by further aid from central bankers, exports rose — and we scraped through with a surplus of £40 million on balance of payments for 1966. The rise in prices was checked. All this had been achieved with a very small increase in unemployment. the rate for 1966 was still only 1½ per cent. Predictions for 1967 by government and other economists were optimistic: a big balance of payments surplus was forecast and it looked as though we were on the way out of our difficulties and this time without the large increase in unemployment that had accompanied previous surpluses.

But 'severe restraint' was harder to operate than 'freeze'. Workers whose promised rises had been held back in the freeze were now allowed to receive them. Two unexpected events, the Arab—Israeli war, which closed the Suez Canal and put up the cost of our imports of oil, and the protracted dock strike hit our balance of payments. A series of unfavourable Trade returns in the autumn months* set off yet another run on the £. The government on 20 November 1967 was forced to devalue the £.

Devaluation reduces the price of our goods abroad and makes exporting easier. It increases the price of imports and therefore tends to reduce them. Both actions help our balance of payments. But, over a period of time, it sends up prices at home as the cost of imports rises. To reduce demand in the home market and release goods for export the government increased taxation and cut its own spending. This reduced spending resulted in more unemployment: by December 1967 it was up to 500,000 or about 2½ per cent. The government refused to ease up on its restrictions, as previous governments had done, because this had merely stimulated the home market and led to further balance of payments difficulties. The unemployed would be absorbed, they said, as exports expanded. What was needed was an 'export-led boom'.

Deflationary restrictions held back the economy. Instead of the steady 3½ per cent increase in output each year forecast by the National Plan, output increased by less than 2 per cent in 1966 and a little more than 1½ per cent in 1967 [2]. Production was expected to increase by 3½ per cent in 1968 thanks to the big increase in exports that, it was expected, would follow devaluation.

Incomes restraint was still necessary, said the government [3]. Total increases were not to exceed 3½ per cent. For the first time dividends were subject to the same legal restraint. Trade unionists complained that rises of 3½ per cent would not be sufficient to cover

* These were subsequently found to be much less unfavourable than was thought at the time, due to a miscalculation.

the anticipated increase in prices (following devaluation) of 5 per cent in the year. It was regrettable, said the government, but unavoidable. There would have to be a fall in the standard of living in 1968 of 1—1½ per cent. It was the price of devaluation. We had been living beyond our means and it was necessary to tighten our belts until we were paying our way.

In fact, the standard of living did not fall. Prices went up by the anticipated 5—6 per cent but average earnings went up by 8.6 per cent in 1968. Those who were subject to restraint and secured increases of 3½ per cent only suffered a lower standard. Those who got larger increases (by promising greater productivity or by sheer market pressure) benefited. Private consumption went up by 1.2 per cent in real terms compared with a forecast fall of 1.9 per cent [4]. Partly because of this higher level of consumption, imports were much higher than forecast and slowed down progress towards the achievement of a substantial surplus on balance of payments, despite a satisfactory increase of 18 per cent in exports. A further satisfactory feature in 1968 was the rise in output of 4 per cent. This improvement enabled the Chancellor to announce in his 1969 Budget speech the gradual removal of legal restraints on wage and price increases which, he said, by their very nature, could not be more than short-term remedies. But voluntary restraint was still necessary.

The government continued to hold the economy on a tight rein in 1969. Taxation was maintained at the existing very high levels. The process of 'deficit financing' (see p. 129) was reversed: the government raised more in taxation than was spent on current and capital account, in order to mop up some of the excess spending power which contributed to inflation. Reductions were not possible, said the Chancellor. Had earnings been more restrained in 1968 the Budget could have been easier. We could not have it both ways, in large increases *and* tax reductions [5]. The government was determined that the advantages of devaluation were not to be lost by a no doubt popular, but nevertheless premature, easing up. The country was rewarded by a record surplus of £450 million on balance of payments in 1969 [6]. But there were still serious difficulties. Output increased at only 3 per cent in 1969 but average earnings had gone up by 9 per cent. There was a record rise in the retail price index of over 6 per cent. Unemployment remained at 2½ per cent.

In his Budget speech in April 1970 Mr Jenkins, the Labour Chancellor of the Exchequer, outlined three essential requirements of economic policy: first, that growth of total demand (i.e. spending by individuals, businesses and the government) must be kept in line with increase in productive potential: second, that industrial investment must be improved, and third, that we must remain competitive abroad.

He noted that all the countries maintaining a high level of employment and a high rate of growth had suffered from rising prices but warned that

> the illusion that money incomes can be pushed up by the kind of figures that have become common in industrial bargaining recently, without harmful effects . . . is a dangerous one. Everyone concerned with wage settlements should understand that if we are to achieve the reasonable stability of prices which is necessary for a sound economy and a healthy social framework, incomes cannot for long continue to rise at this recent rate.

He responded cautiously to demands from the TUC General Council and others that he should initiate a substantial expansion of the economy. His measures aimed to increase the rate of growth from 3–3½ per cent. There was a small reduction of income tax and 2 million people were relieved of payment altogether. It was a Budget for the future with no concessions to electioneering popularity.

15.2 The general election of 1970

A general election followed in June. Conservatives concentrated on the less successful aspects of Labour's record, particularly their failure to control rising prices, which, they said were the result of irresponsibly high wage demands, tolerated, if not actually encouraged, by the Labour government. 'The £ in your pocket is worth only 14s 7d' they repeated continually. Labour pointed to the record balance of payments surplus as the basis for a sound expansion of the economy. Conservatives drew attention to the cost of this success: unemployment at record high levels and productivity at record low ones. And the balance of payments, they said, had passed its peak. Conservatives promised to cut income tax to restore the incentive to hard work, and to reduce indirect taxes where these put up prices. They promised to cut wasteful government expenditure and concentrate social security spending where it was most needed. They would end government interference in industry, get the economy moving and thus reduce unemployment. While maintaining our democratic system of collective bargaining, they would, nevertheless, tackle industrial relations and the wages explosion.

Labour critics noted many contradictions in these proposals. The promised reductions in taxation could be grossly inflationary, they said; cutting government expenditure meant an impoverishment of the social services; concentrating social welfare 'where it was most needed' involved a return to the means-test; 'tackling the wages explosion' was a euphemism for an attack on wages and the trade unions.

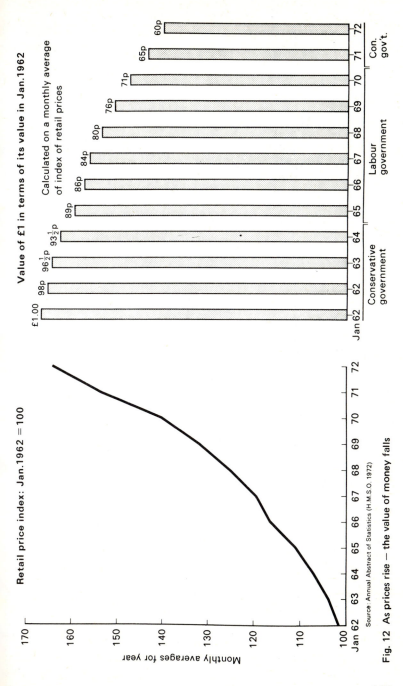

Fig. 12 As prices rise — the value of money falls

Value of £1 in terms of its value in Jan.1962

Calculated on a monthly average of index of retail prices

Retail price index: Jan.1962 = 100

Monthly averages for year

Source: Annual Abstract of Statistics (H.M.S.O. 1972).

143

The electorate, late in the campaign, possibly because it thought Labour singularly quiet on its own remedies, turned to the Conservatives, who won with a comfortable majority of thirty seats over all other parties. The new Conservative Prime Minister was Mr Edward Heath.

15.3 The Conservative government of 1970

The Conservatives under Mr Heath came in with the determination to show that, whatever had been said of other post-war Conservative governments, and the difficulty to distinguish them from their socialist opponents, *they* would be different.

First, they would no longer interfere as a government in business affairs: and particularly, they would not support the 'lame ducks' of industry, the shipyards and aerospace firms, into which, they said, the Labour government had poured too many millions of the taxpayer's money. These firms must now learn to stand on their own feet.

Second, they would introduce an Industrial Relations Bill to establish a legal framework for industrial bargaining and make explicit a code of conduct for employers and workers alike. They would stand firm against inflationary wage demands and thus get at the source of price rises that had spiralled under Labour.

Third, they would tackle the system of taxation to restore incentive, encourage industrial investment and promote efficiency in industry. In particular, they would reduce taxation on incomes.

Fourth, they would introduce selectivity into the social services, stop the provision of free services to those well able to pay and concentrate help where it was most needed.

Ministers began with a rigorous examination of departmental expenditure and reduced government 'interference' in business by abolishing the Prices and Incomes Board, the Industrial Reorganisation Corporation, the Productivity Council, the Consumer Council and the Land Commission. Negotiations for entry into the European Economic Community were begun. The Industrial Relations Bill was given priority in Parliament and passed all stages by August 1971 despite vigorous opposition from the Labour Party and loud protests from the trade unions (see Chapter 7). The government's policy of resisting 'excessive' wage demands met some success as Local Authority manual workers settled in November 1970 and Post Office workers in January 1971, after costly strikes, for little more than they had been offered originally.

But in applying its 'lame-ducks' policy to industry the government ran into some trouble. The first of its 'lame-ducks' was none other than Rolls-Royce and in refusing to put up the money that

Workers having mass-meeting during their work-in at Upper Clyde shipyards

company needed, forced it into liquidation: a part of the firm was nationalised (temporarily) and production of the RB 211 engine financed until the contracts with Lockheeds of the USA were renegotiated. A second shock occurred when the government refused to go on financing Upper Clyde Shipbuilders. The prospect of greatly increased unemployment on Clydeside — with an existing above average rate of unemployment — led to much public concern and many schemes for the future of UCS, most involving a reduction in its activities, were canvassed. The government insisted that it must stand on its own feet. The workers 'occupied' the shipyard, refused to consider any of their members redundant and supported them by levies on those still receiving pay. Eventually the government injected some £30 million into the industry. (It had originally jibbed at £6 million.) It claimed that its actions had forced the companies concerned to reorganise and that money had not been forthcoming until the companies had put themselves on a sound financial base.

In its 'management' of the economy the government moved cautiously. The Chancellor's first Budget in October 1970 reduced income tax by 6d in the £ (2½ per cent), and announced £1,600 million saving in government spending by 1974—5. Mr Barber was, in fact, allowing very little additional demand to flow into the economy. Though in different words the message was the same as Mr Jenkins': 'You cannot have it both ways'; in greatly increased incomes and in tax reductions. Charges for prescriptions, optical and dental treatment were increased, free milk for children over seven was stopped, the subsidy of 6d (2½p) a pint of cheap welfare milk was removed and the price of school meals increased. However, total expenditure on the social services and education was to go up and families with low incomes helped by a new cash allowance, the Family Income Supplement.

In his Budget of April 1971 Mr Barber again moved cautiously. Again the amount of demand injected into the economy was small. Again the need to de-escalate wage demands was emphasised. Retirement pensioners were promised a substantial increase from the following September and income tax allowances for children were increased.

By July 1971 unemployment had risen to 800,000. Both the Confederation of British Industry and the TUC General Council had been pressing the government to increase the rate of growth in the economy: the government's caution was due to its fear that increased demand would encourage inflation. However, in July 1971 the Confederation of British Industry reported that some 200 of the largest firms in the country were willing to restrict price increases over the next twelve months to a maximum of 5 per cent. In response to this gesture and because the rate of increase of money incomes had levelled off Mr Barber offered his third packet: purchase tax on all articles was reduced substantially and all hire-purchase restrictions removed. Mr Barber estimated that these and previous measures would increase the rate of growth in the economy from 4–4½ per cent over the previous year and halt the rise in unemployment. The last expectation, however, was not fulfilled and unemployment rose to 970,000 by January 1972.

In January 1972 the miners challenged the government's policy of wage restraint, demanding a substantial rise, striking and picketing aggressively to ensure that no coal reached the electricity generating stations. A State of Emergency was declared, electricity rationed; industrial activity slowed down and up to 1½ million men were laid off. The government set up an inquiry under Lord Wilberforce which recommended exceptional and large increases in wages for the miners. The government laid stress on the 'exceptional' character of the settlement and urged the need for continued wage restraint.

In his Budget speech of April 1972, Mr Barber claimed that, thanks to the government's measures and the actions of the CBI in limiting price increases, the pace at which prices had been rising had been reduced from 10 to 5 per cent per annum. Similarly, the average level of wage increases had fallen significantly. Accordingly, he felt able to reduce taxation by some £1,400 million, giving all income-tax payers £1 a week each in tax reductions. This massive injection into the spending capacity of the people was designed to boost industrial activity, reduce unemployment and increase the production of goods and services by 5 per cent over the previous year. We were back in the era of massive deficit financing (see p. 129), the government spending far more than it raised in taxation, borrowing huge sums to do so.

However, the government's policy of 'sitting on' wage demands had been breached. Following the miners the dockers had secured an advance and other settlements were at a high level. Accordingly, the government called into consultation the TUC General Council and the Confederation of British Industry to discuss means to contain inflation. Although all parties agreed on the aim – containing inflation – they differed as to its cause and the means to contain it. The TUC emphasised that wage-costs were less than half of total costs and were not the sole cause of rising prices; that wage increases accompanied by increased productivity were not inflationary; and that the government's own acts in forcing up council house rents under the Housing Finance Act and food prices by EEC entry had contributed to inflation. The government held to its view that a major cause of inflation was 'excessive' wage demands, i.e. increases in excess of the nation's increased production. It sought a voluntary agreement on means to control incomes, prices and profits in continuing discussions with the TUC and the CBI.

By the summer of 1972 agreement had not been reached and

wage settlements and retail prices were again rising fast: average earnings were up 15–17 per cent on the previous year and retail prices up by 8 per cent. Accordingly the government decided that it must act. On 6 November 1972 it announced a standstill on incomes and prices to be followed in April 1973 by a second phase when rises would be limited to £1 a week plus 4 per cent on total wage bills in any firm, the allocation of this sum among the various grades to be negotiated between trade unions and employers, with the claims of low-paid workers given priority. At the same time, prices and profits were to be rigidly controlled. Phase Three, to follow in the autumn of 1973, was to be the subject of prior negotiations and have the aim of establishing a fairer system of rewards and a means for the settlement of incomes and prices that avoided inflation.

The government claimed that its policy of freeze and restraint differed from that of the previous government: it was more flexible, gave more scope for collective bargaining, and was more likely to succeed because it was instituted in a period of economic expansion.

In his Budget speech of March 1973 the Chancellor claimed that his expansionist measures had achieved the growth of 5 per cent anticipated and unemployment had fallen to 700,000. He planned a Budget that would continue expansion at the same rate but warned that he would take action to moderate demand if need be.

Some economists, notably Peter Jay, Economics Editor of *The Times*, thought that the Chancellor should put the brakes on at once (see article in *The Times*, 7 May 1973) [7]. High government expenditure and massive 'deficit financing' had gone on too long. Pursued beyond the point of full employment it would result in balance of payments difficulties and further very serious inflation. Other economists thought that the necessity to put on the brakes would arise in 1974 or 1975.

Many Conservatives were worried by the government's policy of controlling the economy through the Budget, in continuing to subsidise firms in difficulty and in 'interference' in the interplay of market forces by controls (more strict even than under a Labour government) to contain inflation. It violated so many of their cherished beliefs. And it was particularly disappointing after the government's initial clear cut break with previous socialist policies.

The Labour Party also had its worries. It was not sufficient to exploit the Conservative government's economic difficulties (so very like its own) nor to make fun of its frequent reversals of policy. The Labour Party itself needed a new policy. Why had it lost the election? Should it now be seeking a more definitely socialist programme?

These worries turned the attention of the party faithful to the purists on both sides, the keepers of the parties' consciences who had been warning of the danger of departure from established principles.

Their warnings will be noted in the next chapter: they show us what the parties would like to do given a fairer economic climate. They point, also, to the differences that still exist between the parties despite similarities in some spheres of action.

Questions *for discussion and action*
1.   Note *(a)* the similarities, and *(b)* the differences between the actions of Labour and Conservative governments as outlined in these chapters.
2.   Mention any action that the Labour government wished to carry out but was prevented from doing by economic circumstances. Mention any action that the Conservative government wished to carry out but was prevented from doing by economic circumstances.
3.   *To Conservatives:* A. Consider the argument that says that all governments should control the economy on Keynesian lines to avoid the curse of mass unemployment. To what extent is this compatible with the Conservative belief that governments should not interfere in business affairs?

         B. What considerations would you take into account in deciding to denationalise an industry?

To Socialists: A. Consider the argument that says that Keynesian policies enable us to control the economy sufficiently and that further nationalisation is unnecessary.

         B. Name any industry that you still think should be nationalised. Give specific reasons.
4.   Consider the proposition that 'We expect too much from our governments'.
         Do you think it is true that the electorate 'wants it both ways'? (pp. 141 and 146).
         If you think that the electorate is economically irresponsible can you suggest ways in which it can be helped to become more responsible?

Chapter 16

Critics on the Right and Left: The party purists

CONSERVATIVE

16.1 A failure of leadership

During its period out of office from 1964 to 1970 the Conservative Party was subject to severe criticism from many of its members. They thought that in previous periods of office Conservative governments had pursued too 'socialist' a policy, interfering in the economy, introducing economic planning, accepting socialist ideas about the extent of government provision in the social services. Lord Coleraine wrote [1]:

> There has been a failure of leadership, [the leaders have] repeated the shibboleths of the hour, condemning what it is fashionable to condemn and praising what it is fashionable to praise. They have accepted, almost without question, the idea of the omni-competent state and that it is within the power of governments to meet what is called, in the cant of the day, 'the revolution of rising expectations' . . .
>
> The charge that can be levelled against the Conservatives today is not so much that they accepted the prevailing ortho-doxies without question as that they did nothing themselves to influence them. They did nothing to form the climate of opinion: they learned only how to live with it.

An exception has been Mr Enoch Powell, who has marked himself off from the orthodox leadership of the Conservative Party by a series of speeches attacking socialist theory, particularly that concerned with economic planning and the socialist control of industry. By implication he has attacked, also, the established Conservative leadership for adopting socialist or semi-socialist methods. Although many Conservatives refuse to recognise Mr Powell's leadership and some students, angered by his views on immigration, refuse to listen to him at all, his opinions are clearly influential, especially within his own party.

16.2 Belief in capitalism

Mr Powell has said [2] :

> We believe in capitalism. When we look at the astonishing national achievements of the West, at our own high and rising standard of living, we see these things as the result, not of compulsion or government action or the superior wisdom of a few, but of that system of competition and free-enterprise, rewarding success and penalising failure, which enables every individual to participate by his private decisions in shaping the future of his society. Because we believe this, we honour profit competitively earned; we respect the ownership of property great or small: we accept the differences of wealth without which competition and free enterprise are impossible.

Given the freedom to spend our money as we wish, runs the argument, our spending, through the operation of 'the market', ensures that the economy satisfies the desires of the community, because the firms that produce what we want prosper, capital flows into them and they expand and take on more labour; firms that produce what we do not want contract and go out of business.

16.3 Impracticability of planning

Mr Powell, lamenting that the first exercise in national economic planning was undertaken by his own party, the Conservatives (see p. 137), asserts that planning cannot work. Who can foresee the future? Who, for example, could have anticipated the discovery of North Sea Gas? Yet this discovery threw out the 'plans' for gas production and for future investment in the gas industry. Of course, the danger is that once the 'plans' have been prepared, the planners will want to stick to them, to force events to fit the plan rather than adjust the plan to fit events. And if the plan is a government plan, adjustment will be even slower.

But Mr Powell's sharpest comments were directed against the Labour Party, which promised a more vigorous prosecution of National Planning and 'teeth' for the National Economic Development Council.

He quoted the Labour Party's election document 'Signpost for the Sixties' (p. 13).

A National Plan, with targets for individual industries — especially the key sectors which produce the tools for expansion — would enable every industry and undertaking, publicly or privately owned, to plan its own development with confidence in the future. . . . Once the plan has been laid down, the full resources of the government would be needed to make sure that it was carried out industry by industry.

If this means anything, said Mr Powell, it means that the government would use its full power to make sure that the 'plan' was carried out. But NEDC's target for the motor industry was a growth of 40 per cent between 1962 and 1966 or an average of 9 per cent a year. In fact, the motor industry increased output by 26 per cent in 1963, three times as fast as the 'Neddy' model allowed for.

Mr Powell continued [3]:

By now, therefore, a policy of 'giving Neddy teeth' must have acted to curb the excessive rise in the production of the British motor-car industry — either by rationing of steel and other raw materials or by prescribing maximum limits of output . . . that is what mandatory planning means.

If we reject this we fall back on planning without teeth — indicative planning, with a 'model' composed of 'estimates' instead of a plan composed of targets. But if no one is going to enforce the plan if anyone diverges from the targets it really means that people are going to do what they were going to do anyway — so what is the point of the plan?

16.4 Reliance on the market

No, says Mr Powell, we must rely upon the 'market', a marvellous mechanism that ensures continuing efficiency in the economy and enables us to exercise free choice. It is 'the most wonderful computer the world has ever known. This is the computer into which are fed the whole time millions of facts not only from this country but from all round the globe. The answers tumble out from it in an unending stream; it tells us all the time what is most advantageous to import and export . . . it tells us what can be produced economically and competitively and in what quantity and where'. In place of this mechanism, socialists wish to place an Economics Minister, 'sitting at the centre of a bureaucratic web, determining in detail the activity and destiny of the 50 million souls in this island' [4].

To the socialist argument that the free economy failed to produce those happy results but severe unemployment and poverty amidst plenty in the inter-war years and that in consequence (to quote the Labour Party's manifesto 'Signposts for the Sixties') 'the community must equip itself to take charge of its own destiny and no longer be ruled by market forces beyond its control' but must rely on social ownership of industry and socialist planning, Mr Powell replied [5]:

Controlling our destiny is a fine sounding phrase. . . . They [the socialists] mean that the government, in the name of 'the community' will see that we produce what they think ought to be produced and not what we want to buy; that their preferences and not ours, their priorities and not the consumers' priorities, shall determine the direction of the national effort. Since 'market forces' as they call them — price, profit and loss, supply and demand — will no longer direct the action of men and women in a socialist Britain, they will be directed by another hand. That hand can only be the State's, which in practical, concrete terms means government decisions, applied in detail by commissions, committees, officials, rules, orders and regulations.

. . . If those who invest their savings are no longer to be guided by the rate of interest and the prospect of appreciation, then they must be told what to invest in and made to do so. If the owners of brains or physical strength are not to choose the jobs which offer them what they consider the best return, are not to sell their labour in the best market, then they must be told what jobs to take and made to take them. If the manufacturer is not to produce the articles on which he anticipates the best profit, in consequence of the consumer's demands for these, then he must be told what to manufacture and in what quantities and to what quality and made to comply.

This is what is meant by the community 'equipping itself to take charge of its own destiny and no longer being ruled by market forces beyond its control.' The equipment is nothing less than the full panoply of the authoritarian state.

The government, says Mr Powell, *has* an economic function — to maintain money demand in balance with production — which requires it to limit the extent to which it finances its spending by borrowing from the banking system. But, continues Mr Powell [6], Conservative governments should now make a break with past semi-socialist policies. All nationalised industries should be denationalised and put under private ownership. State intervention in private industry by the Economic Development Committee and other bureaucratic organisations should cease. Attempts to move industry to the distressed or 'development' areas is wrong. Employers should go where efficiency demands: the government should help workers to move to the jobs. The control of rents and housing subsidies that have distorted the housing market must be ended.

Above all, says Mr Powell [7],

Our reasons for upholding the free economy of capitalism are not merely, perhaps not even mainly, material ones. We believe that a society where men are free to take economic decisions for themselves — to decide how they will apply their incomes, their savings, their efforts — is the only kind of society where men will remain free in other respects, free in speech and thought and action. . . .

16.5 The hoax of the Welfare State

Lord Coleraine echoes many of Mr Powell's arguments but particularly attacks the attitude of the Conservative leadership to the Welfare State. He calls for a radical new approach. For while socialists genuinely believe that a welfare service based on ability to pay is wrong because it leads to inequalities, the Conservative sees a society based on universally provided free services as

positively degrading in itself. Its members, in his view, are not to be regarded as mature human beings, able to shoulder responsibility and with a capacity for self development, but rather as eternal children, for whom the necessities of life are provided by an indulgent parent while they themselves are left with a little pocket-money to be spent on such gewgaws as washing machines, television sets, betting shops or pop records. And yet the Conservative, until now, has vied with the socialist in extolling this all-embracing, all pervasive, all-for-nothing idea of social provision [8].

The Welfare State, he asserts, is a hoax. Two-thirds of its expenditure goes to families who contribute more than they receive while those in greatest need are not relieved of their poverty. It was based on assumptions that seemed valid when the Welfare State was conceived; that for the majority there could be no welfare services unless they were provided by the State. No one then saw how the standard of living of the mass of the people would rise so that

every factory would have to provide parking space for its employee's cars, and holidays abroad would be a commonplace for every class except the very poorest.

. . . Long after it had become apparent that the Welfare State was a cruel hoax, that it did little or nothing to relieve poverty and that its effect, so far as the great mass of the population was concerned was to take away more in taxation and contributions than it gave in 'benefits', the leaders of the Conservative Party seemed to be incapable of standing back and re-examining the principles on which social provision by the State is based.

If the majority of people are having things done for them which they are able to do, and would prefer to do, for themselves, but for the burden of taxation which weighs them down and the minority are deprived of adequate help, a solution is clear: let the majority which is in a position to pay for or contribute towards the education of its children, for medical care, for the roof over its head, for its own superannuation, do just those things and be relieved from

> the tribute that the government exacts in order to do, on its behalf, the same things but at greater cost with less variety and with less efficiency. . . .
>
> At the same time, let the minority, the old, the disabled, the lower-paid worker, who cannot afford, no matter to what extent they are relieved of taxation, to buy these things, be provided, not with the services themselves but with the means to pay for them.

There were difficulties in ensuring a basic standard of education, of medical care, and pensions for all. Making up family incomes to a minimum level carried with it the danger that the recipients would not help themselves. But in terms of personal satisfaction, in spending one's own money on one's own family, in simplification of the tax system, in giving real help to the aged, sick and handicapped, the scheme was necessary.

16.6 An exciting Tory reappraisal

Another root-and-branch critic of post-war Conservative policy is Mr Peregrine Worsthorne. The Tory Party, he asserts [9], 'has accepted the Labour Party's basic aim of a classless society'. They must now abandon 'egalitarian social priorities that have their roots in the guilt and shame of the 1930s' and adopt 'new priorities relevant to the 'sixties and 'seventies'.

The one abiding aim of the Tory Party down the centuries has been the establishment and maintenance of a governing class — men and women concerned with the well-being of the State and the good ordering of a free society. The Tory Party has been silent about this: they must now 'mention the unmentionable; it means arguing the case for property, privilege, inherited wealth, private education, for all those aspects of a social system enabling the few to live in a superior style which cuts them off from, and raises them above, the mass . . .' for, 'unless those in positions of authority are endowed with wealth and social status and the special kind of magnetism associated with a privileged style of life, they will not be able to exercise authority effectively and well'.

These writings echo earlier Tory beliefs in the need for an hierarchical society and for an élite (p. 111) and should provide, in Worsthorne's words 'a period of exciting Tory reappraisal'.

To sum up:

Mr Powell argues for an untrammelled free enterprise system and an end to government planning and interference in business.

Lord Coleraine argues for the dismantling of State welfare services and for massive cuts in taxation to enable us to provide our own education, health and superannuation.

Mr Worsthorne wants an open declaration in favour of an unequal society led by an élite.

These are extreme views and will provoke counter arguments from the more orthodox, undoctrinaire Conservatives who pride themselves on their practical approach to politics. Questions appear here, then, rather than at the end of the chapter.

Questions *for discussion (mainly for Conservatives)*
1. To what extent have the views expressed in this section — written before the Conservatives returned to office in 1970 — influenced the actions of the Conservative government since?
   Give specific examples. Consider whether or not the actions were successful.
2. What are Mr Powell's objections to government planning? If planning is so impracticable, why do both parties attempt it?
3. Is the criticism that reliance on 'the Market' did not work in the inter-war period and therefore would not work today, valid? Previous chapters show that government intervention on Keynesian lines, attempted by all post-war governments, is not easy.
   What advantages have flowed from it?
   What disadvantages have flowed from it?
4. Do you think it inevitable that 'planning' must lead to a completely authoritarian State, as Mr Powell suggests?
   Mr Powell frequently 'takes arguments to their logical conclusion'.
   What are the advantages and disadvantages of this form of reasoning?
5. Lord Coleraine suggests that because the majority of people pay

more in taxes and contributions than they receive in benefits, the Welfare State is a 'hoax'.

Do you agree?

Would it be equally true to describe the scheme as one where:

(a) All receive benefits in accordance with needs;

(b) The cost of services enjoyed by those who cannot pay is shared by the majority.

If this is correct, would you call the scheme a 'hoax'?

6. Assuming that all societies need 'leaders', do you think that they should have the privileges that Mr Worsthorne suggests?

7. Do you think that the critcisms made of the Conservative leadership that they have adopted too many of their opponents' ideas is just?

Is there anything wrong in adopting your opponents' ideas? (There are, of course, dangers.) What are the dangers?

8. Refer to question 3 on p. 149 and recall the answer you gave when discussing it.

Now that you have read the views of the purists on your side do you still agree with the answer you gave when discussing it previously?

9. Invite your local Conservative Association to send speakers who differ on some of the issues discussed in this section to put their views before you.

SOCIALIST

The Labour Party, being the party of dissent, protest, change, has a larger number of critics within and without its ranks than any other party. These vary very considerably in the 'purity' of their socialist faith.

16.7 Academic critics

A number of academics, many of them university economists, who were called in to advise Labour Ministers between 1964 and 1970, have put their views in *The Labour Government's Economic Record, 1964–70* [10]. Their chief criticism is that in attempting to plan the economy and achieve some movement towards greater equality in society the Labour government was handicapped by woolliness of aim, by the political decision to avoid devaluation of the £ at all costs (no doubt from the fear that Labour would be labelled as the party of devaluation, having devalued the £ in its previous period in office), from an excessive economic orthodoxy (to sustain the confidence of the City and business) and from economic nationalism.

These critics say that the Labour government should have devalued the £ earlier, then expanded the economy and from the proceeds financed both increased personal incomes and improved social services and overseas aid. These critics appear to accept the mixed economy, ask for no really fundamental change in economic organisation, just clearer and better informed policies and more efficient administration.

16.8 Fabian critics

Fabian critics take Hugh Gaitskell's definition that 'socialism is about equality' as their text and use this as the touchstone of their criticism of the Labour government, 1964—70 [11]. They call for a much more thoroughgoing research into the country's social problems and a more rational approach to policymaking to achieve the desired end of greater equality.

Specifically, they say that little was done to improve the *relative* position of low-paid workers and those in receipt of pensions or social security during Labour's period of office. Low-income families should not only share in the rising prosperity of the community: if inequalities are to be reduced they must have a larger than average share in any improvement. The Fabians' own statistics (p. 16) show that this was, indeed, achieved in a modest way. Labour increased expenditure on pensions, social security and family allowances by 80 per cent between 1964 and 1970. Much of this was absorbed by the increased numbers of old people in the community and increased unemployment. Nevertheless, while the real take-home pay of the average wage earner rose by 10 per cent in this period, the real value of the single pension rose by 14 per cent and benefit for the unemployed man with three children rose by 16 per cent. Fair enough, say the critics. But nothing like good enough.

16.9 Left – Socialist – Marxist critics

More radical critics take the Marxist standpoint. They reject mere reforms and look for the complete transformation of society on socialist lines. They include a number of trade union leaders, some Members of Parliament and groups outside the Labour Party such as the New Left. Beyond these, again, are the International Socialists and the

Maoists. The British Communist Party is in a somewhat questionable position. Its close ties with the Russian and Eastern European Communist Parties have made it suspect and many Marxists say that their policy is reactionary.

Many of these radical critics concede that standards of living in Britain have improved in the post-war years. However, they find the present situation unacceptable. First, the *share* of the national income going to wage and salary earners has changed little since the 'thirties. Secondly, wealth remains very unequally divided: the top 10 per cent of the population still owns 80 per cent of all private property. Its possession confers immense power on the owners, including the ability to create more personal wealth without working, to live on capital gains, and to buy an undue proportion of housing, health provision and education that leaves the rest of the people the poorer. Pension and social security payments, say the critics, for most of the time fail to keep pace with the general rising standard so that the poorest section of the community falls continually behind. The National Health Service (the post-war Labour government's attempt to establish a new standard of communal care) has been starved of resources and is in danger of becoming a second-class service — second to that obtainable by people with money to pay.

Our education system, say these socialist critics, reflects the class system of society. There is the fee-paying sector where, in private preparatory and (so-called) public schools, the sons of the wealthy have an education which enables them to take their places at the head of family businesses and obtain positions of influence in the City, in industry and in government service irrespective of their abilities. Below them, in the public sector, are the grammar schools preparing the brighter members of the middle class for managerial positions, for scientific technology, for the professions. Below again are the schools and technical colleges preparing the skilled, semi-skilled and unskilled manual workers. There is a hierarchy of schools to match the social hierarchy. Grammar school pupils have 70 per cent more spent on them than secondary modern pupils. Educational opportunity, though improved over the last twenty-five years, is still largely determined by social class. Still only ½ per cent of the children of unskilled and semi-skilled workers go to a university — the same as in the 1930s and 1940s; whereas some 14½ per cent of the children of professional, managerial and intermediate occupational groups do so, compared with 4 per cent in the 1930s.

A socialist policy, say the critics, would provide a fully comprehensive public education system to which all children should go, irrespective of social class: the private sector would be abolished.

Why did the Labour government not tackle these problems

radically when in power from 1964 to 1970? Because, say the critics, its economic policy was based on the false belief that an 80 per cent capitalist economy — with a mere 20 per cent nationalised — could be managed on Keynesian lines to produce an increasing output of goods and services from which improved social services and higher living standards could be financed. But this could not happen in a highly competitive capitalist world, say the critics, as the Labour government soon discovered, when tackling the massive balance of payments deficit bequeathed to it by the previous Tory government. First, we were under intense pressure in world markets from United States competition. Second, US capital had penetrated the United Kingdom and creamed off the most profitable home and export markets. Third, British financiers had 'borrowed short and lent long' and the government were caught in their international financial difficulties. Labour, in its efforts to keep the system going without making fundamental changes, held back the standard of living of the workers, found itself in conflict with the unions and had insufficient resources to remedy the deficiencies in housing, health, education and pensions.

The Labour government, say these critics, should have taken strong steps to meet the balance of payments crisis even if this had involved a wide control of City institutions. Private overseas investments should have been nationalised (that is, bought up compulsorily by the government) to pay off short-term debts incurred by our speculating financiers. Hot money from abroad should have been refused, long-term investment overseas strictly controlled. At home a really socialist government would have moved quickly to bring the whole process of production and investment under control, bringing in the workers to participate in the process.

To end inequalities of wealth a steeply graduated wealth tax should have been introduced, the proceeds being used to establish new scientifically based industries in new forms of social ownership. Older industries, like shipbuilding, could have been acquired by the same means. Only when industry is socially owned and planned and the wealth taken by the rich redistributed through taxation should workers be asked to take part in an 'incomes policy' in which all sections of the community, including pensioners, should share. Resources would then be available to rebuild the Health Service expand education on comprehensive lines and deal with housing as a social service.

None of this will be possible, say the socialist purists, if a future Labour government relies merely on the capacity of the existing economic system to expand: it must be prepared to extend public ownership radically and stand up to the City. Otherwise it will be found, once more, meeting crisis after crisis and losing the support of the people it was elected to serve.

Politics is about power. Socialist governments must take firm control of economic as well as political power if they are to be able to achieve their aims. (This argument has been condensed from the writings of the New Left group, especially those contained in 'May Day Manifesto 1968'. [12])

Questions *for discussion and action*
1. Consider the following criticisms of the purist socialist analyses and policy as outlined:
    (a) The emphasis put on what was *not* done by the Labour government for the social services is useful in preventing complacency but overshadows what *has* been done. The effect on the uninformed reader is to arouse a feeling of hopelessness, leading to a rejection of political action, rather than to act as a stimulus, as the authors intend.
    (b) American 'penetration' in British industry has been an aid rather than a disaster, because (i) American firms in Britain are among the most successful exporters. Although they account for only between 6 and 7 per cent of production they account for between 17 and 18 per cent of manufacturing exports. Ford is Britain's second exporter. (ii) They have put some rocky United Kingdom firms (e.g. Rootes) on their feet. (iii) American investment raises the amount of capital per worker and therefore his ability to produce more and raise his standard of living. (Output per worker is 80 per cent higher in the United States than here because its industry is 'capital intensive'.) (iv) Americans introduce new manufacturing processes and management techniques which improve the efficiency of the firms involved and by competition, that of other British firms: they stimulate takeovers and rationalisation of British industry. Some of the increased profit goes back to the USA but much in increased wages here. (v) Britain benefits from American research.
    (c) The real problem is not how to keep out United States capital but how to develop our own industries (possibly in conjunction with Europe) to meet US competition.
2. Refer to question 3 on p. 149 and recall the answer you gave when discussing it.
    Now that you have read the views of the purists on your side do you still agree with the answer you gave when discussing it previously?
3. Get representatives of the points of view mentioned in this chapter to come and talk about their ideas to your group.

Chapter 17

Problems of the 1970s

Unquestionably, the Conservative Party moved to the Right when in opposition from 1964—70. If the Labour Party is in opposition for long, it, in its turn, may move to the Left. The problem for all parties is to produce a policy that will create enthusiasm among its more militant supporters yet not frighten off the 'middle of the road' elector whose vote is necessary if power is to be secured: and without power, even the purest policy is but words.

What, then, does the averagely well-informed elector look for in a government in the 'seventies? He wants, it is suggested, a modest but steadily rising standard of living and for this he needs a government that will:

1. Maintain a steadily expanding economy with high levels of employment and without recurring balance of payments crises.
2. While maintaining our system of free collective bargaining, ensure that incomes do not rise faster than productivity, thereby contributing to inflation (continually rising prices) with its grave social and economic consequences.
3. Ensure that the nation's wealth is more fairly shared.
4. Provide means for the sick, the aged and the needy to live out their lives in dignity.
5. Look continually at the environment to ensure that, in our efforts to improve our standard of living, we are not befouling it.
6. Ensure that, in our collective efforts to solve these problems, we leave to the individual the maximum area of personal decision.

Party policies will be judged, in all probability, less by the purity of their ideology than by their capacity to produce at least some of these ends.

Questions *for discussion and action*
1. Consider the six items of 'policy for the 'seventies' outlined above.
    To what extent and with what success, have recent governments tackled them?
2. What problems remain unsolved? Have you any ideas about how they could be dealt with?
    Watch the local paper for information on people who claim to be able to do so. If their ideas sound sensible, get them to come and talk to your group.

Chapter 18

The citizen's choice

How sensible is the citizen's choice when faced with the alternatives put before him by the political parties?

It is easy to portray the citizen as ignorant, unduly influenced by unfulfillable promises and appeals to his selfish interests, by slogans and advertisements in which parties sell themselves like packets of detergent. According to this view the solid mass of voters go on voting for their parties out of prejudice and sheer inertia, and elections are decided by the odd 2 million 'floating voters', for the most part 'don't knows' and 'couldn't cares' to whom the parties beam their appeal.

This view is, of course, nonsense. The 'floating voters', for example, are not a fixed group. The 'floaters' at one election are not necessarily floaters at the next: some are people who for a variety of reasons are changing sides, most are people who, again for a variety of reasons, are abstaining this time although they voted last; and many are voting now although they abstained before.

Just what are the voters voting *for*? At a general election they are deciding which party shall be put in power to run the country's affairs. True, they vote for a man (or woman) in their local constituency and hope that the party of their choice has chosen a worthy standard-bearer. But they vote primarily for a party. Possibly — very probably — the election will have been presented as a contest between the Party leaders — say Wilson *v* Heath. Actually, only the people of Huyton were voting for or against Mr Wilson and of Bexley for or against Mr Heath. The question before the electors is, 'Are we to have a Labour government or Conservative?' The elector knows this. He has to decide which is the more competent party to tackle the problems that face

the country at that time and for the next four or five years.
How does he decide? By experience, mainly. Probably he could not explain the precise (and sometimes subtle) differences between the party attitudes on housing, education, social welfare or incomes policy, but he has a general idea of how the parties have tackled these questions in the past. He could not quote the figures for the balance of payments over the last three years but he knows that we cannot live without exports at least sufficient in value to pay for our imports and when things go seriously wrong will accept unpleasant policies, like the 'freezes and squeezes' of 1966 and 1973 and the restraints that followed, if he is convinced that there is no other solution. He may not be able to place Vietnam or Rhodesia or Israel accurately on a map but he knows that what goes on there influences him. He knows that while there are nuclear bombs in the world it is a dangerous place, though he may not be able to follow all the arguments about test-ban and non-proliferation treaties and the balance of international power. He has in his mind an 'image' of what the parties stand for and experience of what succeeding governments have brought him in the way of economic well-being. He knows that the government has to govern and is prepared to give the party of his choice a fair run, though he may differ with it over details. He knows also that he has been consulted and the choice is his. He expects, also, to be kept informed about what is going on. He is better educated than he was thirty years ago and less responsive to scares. He is better informed: thanks largely to radio and television and the better newspapers. Despite all that the cynics say, we have had in recent years stable government, responsible and responsive government and a standard of living that most people in the world would envy, though we have been surprised to learn, in recent years, that many nations in Western Europe have got ahead of us.

This is not to say that we should be satisfied. As our problems become more complicated there is need for a better informed electorate. There is much irrationality in our electoral and governmental processes. The more we can reduce the irrational element the safer we shall be.

18.1 Family influence

Where do we get our first political ideas? Mainly from our family. We grow up among talk about Mr Heath — spoken of respectfully — and that so-and-so Wilson: or alternatively about Mr Wilson (respectfully) and that what's-it Heath. Maybe father is an active trade unionist and there is much political talk. He takes the *Sun* or the *Morning Star* and we also glance at it. Or maybe there is little talk. Occasionally, someone puts down a newspaper and says, 'Tories up to their old tricks again', or

'More strikes about who does what!'. We absorb an atmosphere and an attitude to politics and take the family view for granted — until someone challenges it.

The challenge may come from a persuasive man at work or at the day-release college; from a boy-friend or someone else whose opinion one respects: or it may come from an outrageous statement of the opposing point of view. One is niggled, or outraged into finding out more about one's case. Sometimes we heatedly attack the disturbing point of view — and find ourselves a few days later using those very arguments.

For most of us, though, it is conformity: we adopt and carry forward the family ideas until someone challenges them. For many of us, nothing does. We come from a working-class family, go to a working-class school, taking a working-class job. When we marry we live near our old home, with school friends as neighbours; we may even work in the same place as Dad. Our political ideas will continue to be those of our family.

Or perhaps we may have been bright at school, been encouraged by our parents and gone to a grammar school. Then there was a wider choice of job: a branching out, a challenging environment and perhaps a change of political ideas. Or we may have gone on to a university. Here there was much more political discussion that at home; one's fellow students came from a wider range of backgrounds. In the university atmosphere all assumptions are challenged. Frequently we still stick to the party of our parents but support it with more sophisticated arguments. Father voted Labour because it was 'out for the working class'. We support it because economic planning makes sense. Besides, we have seen that people in this country still do not have equality of opportunity — even in education. Or perhaps our parents were Tories because 'the upper class are better at ruling'. We still think that but add that we need an hierarchical society where merit and hard work are recognised and the élite properly rewarded.

In contrast to this are the 'natural' rebels, always taking the contrary view: up against father, picked on at school, disliked by the boss or foreman, blamed for everything, finding a happy place in the extreme parties of Right or Left, where they see things the right way up — upside down to the rest of us. Many young people, not as extreme as this, have a healthy reaction against 'the establishment'. They question tradition: ask 'Why?' — and often don't get very satisfactory answers.

18.2 Social class

Our political views depend very much on the social class to which we belong. The great bulk of the middle class vote Conservative, while the mass of the working class vote Labour. This has been confirmed by many inquiries and while the figures of party support varied from time to time as party popularity rose and fell, all inquiries revealed the same broad pattern.

Thus an inquiry undertaken by David Butler and Donald Stokes in 1963 [1] showed that of people who classed themselves as 'Middle Class':

79 per cent supported the Conservatives
21 per cent supported Labour.

Of those who classed themselves as 'Working Class':

28 per cent supported the Conservatives
72 per cent supported Labour.

It may be objected that self rating as regards social class is a very unreliable basis. Many researchers nowadays use a classification based on *occupation*. Hence the information given above was re-sorted on the basis of the informants' occupation and the following was revealed*:

Table 1 *Occupation and party support*

Party supported	Occupation					
	Higher manage-ment (per cent)	Lower manage-ment (per cent)	Supervisory, non-manual (per cent)	Lower, non-manual (per cent)	Skilled, manual (per cent)	Unskilled, manual (per cent)
Conservative	86	81	77	61	29	25
Labour	14	19	23	39	71	75
	100	100	100	100	100	100

* Political change in Britain Table 4.7, p. 77.

The broad conclusion is the same and the detail confirms it: the 'higher' the class (according to job) the greater the support for Conservatives: with the reverse for Labour.

An earlier inquiry [2] with a simpler classification into four social classes (based on occupation) makes the tendency even clearer (Table 2, p. 168).

Here we see that the great bulk of the middle class vote Conservative and about two-thirds of the working class vote Labour. Nevertheless, one-tenth of the solid middle class and one-quarter of the lower middle class vote Labour and about one-third of the working class vote Conservative.

Table 2   *Voting and social class (percentages)*

Class	Proportion of population in each class	Conservative	Labour	Others	Total
Solid middle class	15	85	10	5	100
Lower middle class	20	70	25	5	100
Upper working class (manual)	30	35	60	5	100
Solid working class	35	30	65	5	100

From M. Abrams: 'Class Distinction in Britain', in *The Future of the Welfare State*. Conservative Political Centre, 1958.

How do we explain the large working-class vote of the Conservatives: one-third of the whole working class making up half of the total Conservative vote?

There is a historical reason. In the last half of the nineteenth century, when the working class first won the right to vote, there was a Tory—Radical Party, led by Disraeli and Randolph Churchill, made up of the older aristocracy — the landed interest — and supported by the working class, in opposition to the Liberal industrialists, then rising to power on the achievement of the Industrial Revolution. As the industrialists were absorbed into the Conservative Party, the Liberals took over the radical mantle and, with it, much working-class support. But since 1900 the Labour Party, benefiting from divisions within the Liberal Party — especially since the First World War — has risen with the decline of liberalism. According to an inquiry published in 1967 by Eric A. Nordlinger [3], working-class Conservatives today still have much respect for 'their betters'. Asked who they would choose as Prime Minister from two men equal in other respects, one being a peer's son and the other the son of a file-clerk in the Civil Service.

> 41 per cent preferred the peer's son
>
> 25 per cent preferred the clerk's son
>
> 23 per cent said both were equally good.

The replies of Labour supporters to the same question showed that

> 20 per cent preferred the peer's son
>
> 47 per cent preferred the clerk's son
>
> 21 per cent said both were equally good.

Asked the same question in terms of the school attended by these hypothetical candidates for Prime Ministership, with Eton and an excellent grammar school as the deciding factor, of the Tories,

> 48 per cent preferred the Eton man
>
> 22 per cent preferred the grammar school man

22 per cent thought both equally good.

The Labour responses were:

26 per cent preferred the Eton man

44 per cent preferred the grammar school man

18 per cent thought both equally good.

Thus nearly half the manual workers who vote Tory and about one-fifth of those who vote Labour would prefer a peer's son as Prime Minister, 'other things being equal'. Reasons given were that the peer's son had been brought up for responsibility and leadership and had experience of it, whereas the man with the working-class background was inexperienced — still fighting his way up. The public schools were also thought to give a better education and training for leadership. In the Tory voters' eyes those were more important than that the Prime Minister should be 'in touch with ordinary people', which was the reason given by those (the Labour voters) who preferred the clerk's son and grammar school product.

Does the manual worker's experience at his place of work influence his choice of party? Nordlinger noted that the larger the plant at which they worked, the greater was the proportion of Labour voters and the smaller the plant the greater the proportion voting Conservative. But as the larger plants are more heavily unionised, voting behaviour may be more a result of union membership than of plant size. A number of surveys have shown that about three-quarters of manual workers who are trade unionists vote Labour. Whether they vote Labour because they are trade unionists or become trade unionists because they are 'Labour' — have been brought up to be Labour — is not yet known.

Nordlinger's inquiries revealed that about half the Conservative voters in the group he investigated thought that a Conservative government would 'do more to better the lot of the workers than it does for other people', while over a third thought it benefited all classes the same. Almost nine-tenths of the Labour voters thought that their party did 'more for the workers'. Nordlinger estimated that four-fifths of the Labour voters thought that the party would provide them with additional material benefits (like pensions, housing and health services) whereas only one-fifth of Conservative supporters seemed concerned with this factor. Indeed, he estimated that almost one-third of these Conservative-voting manual workers believe that they would be materially better off under a Labour government. Then why do they vote Conservative? Positively, they think that the Conservatives are more efficient, have able leaders, support free enterprise and produce prosperity and generally 'do what is best for the country'. Negatively, they do not trust the Labour leaders, find the party too aggressive and do not agree with nationalisation and planning.

18.3 Men's and women's choices

Returning to more general factors: Jean Blondel [4] quotes figures taken from tables drawn in 1964 by the British Institute of Public Opinion, showing that more men vote Labour than Conservative and considerably more women vote Conservative than Labour: and as women form a larger portion of the electorate than men, this is a material factor: figures are:

Table 3 *Voting by sex*

	Whole sample (per cent)	Con- servative (per cent)	Labour (per cent)	Liberal (per cent)	Others (per cent)	Absten tions (per cen
Sex: Male	48	33	41	9	—	17
Female	52	38	33	13	—	16

However, National Opinion Polls [5] showed that in the general election of 1966 more women intended to vote Labour than Conservative, while Labour's dominance among men was even more marked than is shown above. However, in the 1970 general election (when rising prices were an important issue), it was thought that women returned to their traditional support for Conservatives [6].

18.4 Young and old

Jean Blondel [7] notes that young voters (aged 21—34) tend to vote more heavily for Labour than Conservative, but that older voters tend to turn progressively towards the Conservatives: on the other hand, those of sixty-five and over (? pensioners) vote more heavily for Labour:

Table 4 *Voting and age*

Age	Whole sample (per cent)	Con- servative (per cent)	Labour (per cent)	Liberal (per cent)	Others (per cent)	Absten tions (per cen
21—24	8	26	32	9	—	33
25—34	19	30	37	11	—	22
35—44	20	37	38	11	—	14
45—64	37	39	36	13	—	12
65 and over	16	37	39	8	—	16

The high percentage of abstentions in the young is noteworthy.

18.5 Where people live

The neighbourhood where an elector lives also appears to influence his vote. Thus in a heavily working-class area a *higher proportion of working class* will vote for the Labour Party than in a middle-class area. In a generally strong Labour area, like Wales, a higher proportion of the middle class and lower middle class will vote Labour as well as a larger proportion of working class. When working-class people move out into a 'new town' they cease to be 'solid' Labour. Jean Blondel noted that in middle-class districts in Newcastle-under-Lyme, manual workers were less likely to vote Labour than in working-class districts. This may be because they feel themselves to have moved into the (lower) middle class. Nordlinger's inquiries led him to believe that working-class people (defined by the jobs they do, viz. manual work) who classify themselves as 'middle class' probably because of a sense of economic well-being, often vote Conservative out of a belief that this is the proper thing to do and that Conservative measures are most likely to maintain their well-being.

However, economic well-being alone does not appear to affect a worker's allegiance to Labour. Research among well-paid car workers at Luton in 1963–4 [8], while revealing change in style of living indicated little change in political outlook. The date of the inquiry may be significant. It was a time of nation-wide support for Labour and a similar inquiry at a later date would be needed before firm conclusions can be drawn.

18.6 Party propaganda

To what extent are people influenced by the efforts of the parties to win them over? Is there an increase or a decrease in the appeal to reason at election times or are irrational appeals increasing?

There is no doubt, in the opinion of many observers, that elections are conducted at a higher level than in the inter-war years. We are spared the more extreme appeals to fear that characterised elections in the 1920s and 1930s. In 1924 the proposal of the Labour Party that we should trade with Russia was countered by the publication of the Zinovieff letter, now generally acknowledged to be a forgery, which purported to prove that the Russians were organising revolution in England. The posters showed hairy Bolsheviks with bombs and the caption 'Shaking hands with murder'. The Conservative Party paid

£10,000 for a copy of the letter and no doubt thought it authentic. It was widely publicised and the Labour Party was defeated at the polls.

In 1931 there was the Post Office Savings Bank scare when the National government candidates irrelevantly flourished worthless German mark notes and described the Labour policy as reckless inflation. There was also the statement that citizens' savings in the Post Office were in danger because the money was being used to pay unemployment benefit — 'the dole'. In fact the Post Office Savings Bank had lent money to the Unemployment Fund but this was a normal government financial transaction. How many people thought that their money in the Post Office was in danger we do not know, but Labour was routed at the polls.

In the 1945 general election immediately after the war Mr Churchill tried to make the voter's blood run cold by suggestions that Labour's policy would lead to totalitarianism and the 'Gestapo' — a reference to Hitler's secret police. Casting the mild Mr Attlee, the Labour Prime Minister, in the role of a British Himmler was too much for the British voters to swallow and Labour secured a large majority.

Of course, this kind of exaggeration is not all on one side. The *Daily Mirror*, supporting the Labour Party in 1950, published a cartoon headed, 'Whose Finger on the Trigger', with the innuendo that Mr Churchill would be more likely to take the country into a new war than would the Labour Party: putting over the image of the Conservatives as 'warmongers'. In view of the fact that the Conservatives had been accused of cowardice in *not* making war on Hitler in 1938, this was very unfair. The Conservatives, also, were labelled — at least in people's minds — as the party of mass unemployment. As mass unemployment occurred under both Labour and Conservative governments between the wars and both parties were singularly unsuccessful in curing it, this was hardly rational; of course, Conservatives were in power for most of that time and must accept the major share of responsibility. Further, both parties had pledged themselves to 'maintain a high and stable level of employment' in the post-war years by the adoption of Keynesian policies — which neither party had known how to apply in the inter-war years.

Crude scares are no longer tried, due, no doubt, to the knowledge that the electorate is better educated and better informed, than in former times. But irrational appeal takes different forms. Slogans so generalised as to have no meaning are plastered on the hoardings and in the press. What precisely does 'Let's Go with Labour', the 1964 slogan, mean? Go where? To do what? True, this slogan was often accompanied by statements about what Labour was proposing to do about schools and housing. What, then, was the value of the slogan? Does it imply that the voting public is only capable of absorbing a simple

Let's GO with Labour and we'll get things done

Election poster with slogan

generalised statement, suggesting 'getting somewhere' and not able to absorb detailed points of policy?

The Conservatives' slogan, 'Life's better with the Conservatives: Don't let Labour ruin it', at least had the merit that its opening phrase was something that people could test by experience. But no attempt was made to substantiate the assertion that 'Labour would ruin it' a rather obvious appeal to fear. This was the 1959 message. During the economic setback of 1962—3 the Conservatives were unable to use it because electors would know from experience that it was false. But it was reintroduced in the 1964 campaign as 'Conservatives give you a better standard of living: Don't chuck it away'. Posters showed photographs of happy looking prosperous families, often with a car and an attractive young wife to the fore, with whom it was hoped that the electors could identify themselves. As the campaign progressed there was less text discussing policy, more reliance on picture and slogan. Incidentally, the Conservatives paid over £1 million on advertising in this campaign.

The steel companies and the British Iron and Steel Federation spent £1¼ million campaigning against the proposed renationalisation of their industry by the Labour Party. Richard Rose [9] writes:

> The first series of messages, appearing in November and December 1963, put the case for the steel industry to the attentive élite in lengthy, solid text layouts. The second series . . . was intended for the mass electorate. Advertisements featured photographs of women, children and animals in situations completely unrelated to the steel industry. The text underneath sought to link the illustration to an argument for leaving steel in private hands. For example, a picture of a woman and her children having tea was accompanied by a text captioned, 'Tea and Steel are two of the things we in Britain make rather well.' . . . In the six weeks before the election the Federation sponsored a single large advertisement showing an empty shopping basket; it had the caption 'If they nationalise steel — YOU PAY'.

The result of this campaign appears to have been a slight fall between February and December 1964 (from 28 to 24 per cent) in the percentage of people in favour of nationalising steel and an increase from 50 to 57 per cent in those who opposed. Despite the efforts of the steel companies it was not an issue at the election. The Labour leaders refused to pick up the challenge and the electorate was not interested.

Shall we see more photographs of dogs and happy children in future political campaigning? It is encouraging to read that Mr Wilson vetoed an advertisement prepared for the Labour Party showing a baby being bathed by its mother on the grounds that it was 'beneath the dignity of a political party'; and that a Conservative political television programme that took the form of a 'soap opera' showing the benefits obtained by a typical family under Conservative rule, on the lines of a TV commercial, disgusted some senior Ministers and was criticised in the more responsible press.

As Mr Rose concludes [10]:

. . . advertising a party is different from and far more difficult than advertising a packet of soap. The actions and nature of the soap can be controlled and predicted by the media [advertising] men, whereas the actions of a political party, especially a party in office, cannot.

In the general election of 1966 there were no last-minute scares. The Labour Party, after a short spell with an uncomfortably small majority, was seeking a substantial victory so that it could implement the promises it had made in 1964. It campaigned on the slogan 'You *know* Labour Government works' and emphasised the 'Thirteen Wasted Years' of previous Conservative rule. Its manifesto added very little to the 1964 programme. The Conservatives refused to be drawn on the 'thirteen wasted years' and put forward a constructive new programme.

There were press conferences in the morning and speeches from the leaders at night covering much ground about the economy and the social services (in response to press and radio demands for a fresh issue every day). Two issues 'emerged'. Some trade unionists were alleged to have 'tried and fined' eight members who had refused to join in an unofficial strike and the newspapers carried stories of a hangman's rope hanging above the 'guilty' men. The story was blown up by the press for several days; one accused man was said to be in a state of nervous exhaustion. The 'noose trial' was the subject of many Conservative speeches coupled with demands for changes in trade-union law. The Minister of Labour called for a report on the incident (the noose was later said to have been no more than sky-larking). A few days later another case of fining by trade unionists was featured. Conservative leaders claimed that their proposals would end this 'intimidation'. By the end of the week the press dropped the story and gave little space to the charges that the men suffering from nervous breakdowns had been harried more by reporters than their co-trade unionists. Labour accused the Conservatives of blowing up the issues for political purposes. Butler and King [*op. cit.*], commenting on the issue, think that some Conservatives thought the press campaign had done them no good: when they wanted to discuss trade unions seriously the press had become bored and the real issues were not debated.

The second issue was the European Economic Community which was pressed by the newspapers favouring Britain's entry. Mr Wilson held his fire on this issue for some time and it may be that press interest finally drew him. His speech on it was criticised, but there is evidence that his caution reflected the attitude of the voters.

Reporting, particularly on television, tended to over-emphasise the heckling at meetings because this produced a more vivid news item than the more serious explanations of party policy. There were complaints, too, that the swivelling of cameras and arclights encouraged the more exhibitionist hecklers. The dismantling of cameras after the departure of the guest speakers was criticised by candidates who had to meet this distraction as well as the difficulty of following more experienced orators.

These distractions apart, the election was considered by experienced observers to be one of the most reasonable of recent years. Although some politicians and journalists were said to consider it 'boring' (possibly because they thought the outcome already decided), Gallup Polls showed that rather more voters described themselves as 'very interested' (42 per cent as against 36 per cent in 1964), viewing figures for the party television broadcasts were the highest ever (85 per cent claimed to have seen one or more), and despite the increased coverage given by radio and TV the main news bulletins and special campaign reports held their audiences right through to polling day.

Election campaigns are important sources of political education. As in other spheres, the better the electorate is educated, the more it is prepared to take.

This made the general election of 1970 disappointing. Mr Wilson deliberately 'played it cool', hoping to be returned on the record of the Labour Party in securing a massive balance of payments surplus following devaluation. He refused to take up his opponents' challenges and no interesting issues emerged. This appeared to be paying off as the opinion polls predicted a comfortable majority for Labour. However, Mr Heath fought through to the end, casting doubts on the health of the economy (less favourable balance of payments figures published in the last week of the campaign seemed to support this). Conservatives, assured by private inquiries that the public was genuinely worried over rising prices, and responding to the '£1 only worth 14s 7d under Labour' slogan, hammered away on this point. There was a substantial last minute swing and the Conservatives won by a majority of thirty over all other parties.

Many commentators thought that an opportunity to educate the electorate had been lost. There was little debate on the larger issues, such as Britain's entry into the European Economic Community, on the distribution of the nation's wealth, on means to stimulate economic growth while avoiding inflation, on the future of the social services, on taxation, etc.

It is possible that the Labour Party underestimated the electorate. Alternatively, it may be claimed that it took too high a view of the electorate in not offering it pre-election bribes (its Budget had been tough), and that the Conservative '£1 in your pocket' campaign *was* effective.

The decision, so widely differing from poll forecasts, at least shows that the electorate *does* take note of what is said and *is* open to persuasion.

18.7 Opinion polls

In addition to forecasts at election times, we are familiar with reports in the press and on TV that 57 per cent of the people of X-town are for, 32 per cent against a certain project with the inevitable 11 per cent of Don't Knows.

How is that information obtained?

No one pretends that every citizen in X-town has been questioned. A 'representative sample' is chosen which ideally reflects the social and economic make-up of the population. Thus, if 10 per cent of the population are pensioners, 10 per cent of the sample should be. If 55 per cent are semi-skilled workers in the local engineering works divided as to ¾ male and ¼ female, then the sample should have the same proportions. Clearly, if the sample is too small it will not be able to reflect such fine distinctions and the result will be less reliable. But experience shows that the sample need not be excessively large.

When voting intentions are polled a representative sample may consist of every one-hundredth person on the Register of Electors. If the opinion of schoolchildren is being taken, then the pollsters try to take a cross-section from a number of schools.

The organisations doing public-opinion research in Britain, whose names appear frequently in the newspapers (Gallup Poll, National Opinion Polls), are experienced, use scientific methods and rely for their existence on the reliability of their results. If, for example, their figures of 'intended voting' at an election proved to be wildly at variance with subsequent actual voting, then, unless there was an adequate explanation of last-minute changes of mind among voters, their reputation would be damaged. In the 1970 general election, for example, National Opinion Polls put Labour ahead by 12.4 per cent on the Friday before polling day. Allowing a 3 per cent margin of error, a lead of 9.4 per cent seemed unbeatable. But Labour lost. The Conservatives, informed by a private poll that their propaganda on rising prices ('The £1 in your pocket is only worth 14s 7d') was influencing voters, plugged away on this issue and opinion swung against Labour.

To what extent are people influenced by the polls? There is a suggestion that at election time polls may produce a 'band-waggon' effect. If support is shown to be running strongly towards one party, people join in so as to be with the majority. The polls thus tend to bring about what they predict. Against this it is said that a party that looks like having a walk-over finds that its less responsible supporters do not trouble to vote. This works against self-fulfilment. Because of both of these supposed effects a proposal has been made that the publication of poll results should be prohibited in the week before polling day.

A better safeguard is for people to realise just what the polls are saying (incidentally, they rarely 'predict' election results, merely indicate voting intentions at a certain date beforehand). In February 1973 Mr Douglas, Labour Member for East Stirlingshire and Clackmannan, introduced a Bill into Parliament 'to regulate the publication of public opinion polls to ensure a fair and balanced presentation'. It required the publication of the questions asked, information on the size of the sample and the number of respondents. Additionally, it required that the 'sponsorship' should be made public and the cost of the poll disclosed because sometimes those who paid for the polls 'structured' the questions to get the answers desired. It required, also, the setting up of a committee in the pre-election period to inquire into the accuracy and meaning of polls.

Knowledge of the movement of opinion is useful, especially to people who are actively involved in politics. It helps them plan election strategy. It is interesting, also, to the individual citizen to know what other people think on the issues on which he is making up his mind — provided he makes up his own mind and is not just following the crowd. So long as there is a free press and free broadcasting organisations able to expose malpractices, it is to be hoped that there will be no undue restriction on the publication of poll results: access to information is essential in a democratic society.

Questions *for discussion and action*

1. From the evidence of this chapter, do you think it true to say that politics in this country is 'class-based'?

2. Examine hoardings, newspapers and party political broadcasts and make a list of current political slogans. Consider their rational and irrational aspects.

3. List the main daily and Sunday newspapers: note *(a)* their ownership and *(b)* their political views.
   Examine one 'quality' and one 'popular' newspaper and mark the 'political' items in each. Note their relative weight. Have the papers a political bias?

4. Journalists and politicians use emotionally charged words to persuade people to their view. Note the following examples: complete the list.

Favourable	Neutral	Unfavourable
Statesman	Politician	Party hack
Literature	Leaflet	Propaganda sheet
Consolidation	Diminution	Retreat
Investment	Spending	Extravagance
Economy drive	Cut in spending	Starvation of services
	Policy	
	Campaign	
	Voter	
	Candidate	

5. Note the following use of 'emotive language':

Phrases used about your own party:	Phrases used about your opponents:
Vigorous debate	Acrimonious discussion
Differences of principle	Deep divisions
Earthy commonsense of Mr A	Sophisticated slickness of Mr B
Constant reminder	Repetition ad-nauseam
Mr B's determination to maintain	Mr A's personal obsession with

Watch for similar examples in newspapers and party statements, and keep a scrap-book of them.

6. Cardinal Heenan, writing in *The Times* (25 March 1969), notes the use of the following words and expressions designed to soften the impact of formerly used terms.

Present soft expression	Former stark expression
Underprivileged	Poor
Undernourished	Starving
Permissive morality	Immorality
Handicapped	{ Cripples / Mentally defective
Those suffering from terminal disease	The dying
Abortion	Destruction of life in the womb or killing the unborn child
Euthanasia	Killing incurable patients.

The Cardinal's suggestion is that we mislead ourselves (and others) by the use of these 'soft terms'. Do you agree? Watch for other examples of this practice. (Note how people avoid the words death, pregnant, bastard, kill, steal.)

7. Examine the following paragraphs for emotionally charged language.
   Rewrite them 'straight'.

   (a) From 'Some Principles of Conservatism', by Peter Goldman, Conservative Political Centre, 1s (5p), 1961.

   In every generation there are always whose who, wishing to perfect the social arrangements of the nation, conceitedly suppose themselves able to do so by the light of their naked intellect. They are content to stake their credit and fortunes on a high-sounding panacea, on some flashy slogan to which the whole truth about politics (or economics) may be reduced. Such glib self-confidence can often sound clever and so prove an electoral advantage. But not for long; because the time inevitably arrives when the slogan begins to look hopelessly dated, the panacea is shown in practice to cure nothing or next to nothing, and that particular game is up. 'Nationalisation of all the means of production, distribution and exchange' is only the latest in a long line of exploded fallacies.

   (b) From 'The Social Services 1968', the Labour Party, 9d (4p).

   The Tory Years: . . . After a few years of Tory administration of the education services there seemed to be a retreat on all fronts. Both primary and secondary schools were hideously overcrowded, despite the declared objective of a maximum of forty in a primary class and thirty in a secondary school class in the 1944 Act. The educational building programme was held back. The 1962 School Building Survey showed the state of our schools in horrifying detail. . . . The Tories childishly suppressed their own officially commissioned survey and it was left to the incoming Labour government not only to publish it but to make good the deficiencies it revealed. . . .

   Educational experience has been degraded for the majority of schoolchildren by a decision to give them a separate and unequal system of education. This was a form of educational apartheid which could no longer be tolerated or defended in a society that genuinely wanted to achieve equality of opportunity.

   (The 'straight' versions are less exciting than the original versions. Does this mean that a 'straight' consideration of politics would be boring?)

8. Examine some other pamphlets issued by the party propaganda departments. Note: *(a)* The proportion of space given to attacking their opponents' record, compared with that given to a

statement of their own policy. *(b)* The use of emotionally charged language.

9. Some popular newspapers habitually present politicians, irrespective of party, as figures of fun. (Collect examples.) Do you think that it could lead to a general disillusionment with politics? No doubt they think that their readers enjoy it. Assuming that they do enjoy it, can you give any reasons why people should enjoy thinking ill of the people they have chosen to represent them?

Chapter 19

What can we do about it?

19.1 No man is an island

This book is written in the belief that if we demand (and we do) that the government should act in the multitudinous ways outlined then we should be prepared to take on the responsibilities that are inseparable from citizenship in a democracy: that we should inform ourselves about the problems involved, know what has already been achieved and search out ways of going on from our present position. And having found the way forward, to put in the effort to bring about the changes required. This may mean joining a political party, or a group whose aim is to press for specific changes like the Child Poverty Action Group, or the local parent—teacher association, the local civic society which aims to clean-up ugliness and squalor; to be an active and responsible member of a trade union, students' association, young farmers' club; to take part in one of the many organisations where personal social service can be rendered to people in need: through Youth Service Volunteers, Shelter, Task Force, Oxfam, War on Want; to help immigrants settle-in by teaching them to speak and write English, to welcome them into our associations and homes and at work; to train ourselves for the jobs we shall be called on to do in our working lives.

The person who has read this far may well be convinced that his participation is necessary. But there are many who will still need convincing if they are to be stirred to the minimum participation required if democracy is to continue: and some who, out of the highest motives, will reject the society described here and seek a solution either by opting out, by concentration on membership of a small group or society, on anarchist lines; or by promoting revolutionary action to replace our present — to them — corrupt society.

To take the first: they feel themselves of no account: no one will listen to what they say. They are highly sceptical about politics. They are the apprentices who want to be active in the union but are 'kept out' by the older members. The young men of eighteen to twenty who say, 'I'm a third of the way through my life and look at what I have achieved — nothing. There are no opportunities nowadays.'

To them we must point out patiently that there *are* opportunities today, more than ever before: for choice of job, for training (not in the evenings as some were compelled to do in the old days but on day and block release); for leisure, through sports facilities (the complainant above was learning golf!); for travel, by car and motor bicycle; through holidays with pay. These advances have been won by people who did something about them. New advances will be gained in the same way.

Then there are those who deny any responsibility: 'I didn't ask to be born,' they say. 'I don't owe anybody anything. I am only responsible to myself.' As Mick Jagger* put it when in court on a drug charge: 'What I do with my consciousness is my own affair.' His view is that every man is an island, with the right to organise and conduct his life as he pleases.

But no man is an island. We are social creatures and not only in the sense that we like being with others, but that we are dependent on each other. We inherit our possibilities (for good or ill) from our parents and from their parents: what we do with our inheritance depends not only on ourselves but on the people who nurture us, in infancy, in childhood, in school; it depends on our friends and our jobs and our relations at work, on our neighbours: it depends on what goes on in other countries. As we are influenced by others, so we influence them. We are part of *their* environment. When the bell tolls to announce the death of a neighbour, wrote John Donne, do not send to know for whom the bell tolls: for 'No man is an *Island*, entire of itself; every man is a piece of the Continent, a part of the Main. . . . Any man's *death* diminishes *me*, because I am involved in *Mankind*; And therefore never send to know for whom the *bell* tolls; it tolls for *thee*.' [1].

And just as we are 'members one of another' in the social sense, so we are, or should be, in an economic sense. Here, again, we inherit a 'going concern'. All of us born in the second half of the twentieth century in this island find a vast industrial, commercial and agricultural complex in which each one of us can find a job and because of the equipment at our command can produce and have a share in wealth

* A pop group leader well known in the 1960s and 1970s.

beyond the imagination of earlier times. There is also vast social capital: houses, schools, hospitals, roads, parks, libraries, museums, playing fields, for our use. Granted that the resources are, according to many, unfairly owned, that the produce is unfairly shared: this is not to deny the existence of the inheritance but to criticise our institutions, and our manner of operating them. No one denies that there are great changes to be made. If our arrangements were perfect, this book would have been unnecessary. The point is that we should not deny the existence of our heritage, not neglect it and particularly that we should leave a larger inheritance for those that come after.

What we make of our inheritance depends greatly upon our politics. Here again we are not starting from scratch. Political thinkers, statesmen, politicians, writers, ordinary party workers have left us a body of ideas, a working system, that we should do well to keep in being as a 'going concern'. Conservative thought has given us the idea of an organic society, a growing, changing evolving system. Socialist thought has given us the idea of social concern and responsibility. We shall all put the emphasis in different places but these seem a good starting point from which to move forward.

19.2 The need to protest

There is certainly no place for complacency in this scheme. We must object and protest where we see injustice. And there *is* plenty of injustice — and probably always will be for as we remedy one injustice we uncover another and our sensitivity to injustice will, one hopes, become ever more acute.

Harold Laski [2], a political philosopher of the 1930s, wrote:
Those who accept commands they know to be wrong make it easier for wrong commands to be accepted. Those who are silent in the presence of injustice are, in fact, part authors of it. It is to be remembered that even a decision to acquiesce is a decision and that what shapes the substance of authority is what it encounters. If it meets always with obedience, sooner or later it will assume its own infallibility. . . . Liberty means being faithful to oneself and it is maintained by the courage to resist. . . .

The individual, therefore, is entitled to act on the judgement of his conscience in public affairs. . . . We ought, doubtless, to convince ourselves that the path it indicates is one we have no alternative but to follow. . . . We should remember that civilisation is, at best, a fragile thing and that to embark upon a challenge to order is to threaten what little security it has. It may even be wise, as T. H. Green once put it, to assume that we

Non-violent demonstration

Violent demonstration

should approach the State in fear and trembling, remembering the high mission with which it is charged. . . .

But

Power is not conferred upon men for the sake of power, but to enable them to achieve ends which win happiness for each of us. If what they do is a denial of the purpose they serve; if, as we meet their acts there appears in them an absence of goodwill, or blindness to experience alien from their own, an incapacity imaginatively to meet the wants of others, what alternatives have we save a challenge to power or a sacrifice of the end of our life?

Nevertheless, the means to be employed in challenging power are important. The State, said Laski, is not justified in preventing the expression of opinion or desire: it is justified only in preventing the realisation of desire by violent means.

19.3 The revolutionaries

This brings us to the revolutionaries who, believing our present society to be irremediably corrupt, want to smash it and replace it by a new civilisation, with new customs, new institutions that will enable man to live a life unconfined by the dead practices of the past.

They are prepared to see things worse before they are better: when pressed, they acknowledge that their policies might well produce chaos for a number of years. But then. . . .

Many people can remember the 1930s when there was the misery of mass unemployment — 20 per cent of the entire working population. But even then there were 80 per cent at work. Chaos, now, would mean 80 per cent unemployed and 20 per cent at work. This, surely, must be avoided at all costs. Change, yes (and this book is a plea for change) but always, we may hope, from worse to better.

Of course, revolutionary change appeals, especially to young people. But the new dawn envisaged will not be the golden sunrise of our imagination, viewed from the mountain top, with air like wine and we, hand in hand with our comrades (of the other sex, of course) running down to meet the old. If the revolutionaries have their way we shall be shuffling in the ashes of a burnt-out civilisation.

19.4 Anarchists and the alternative society

Is there no other way than the slow development of political change? Some anarchist groups seek an 'alternative society', built from the living experience of small groups whose members work together to create a microcosm of the new society, where property is held in common, cooperation the rule, and love, not hate, the aim. Will not these communes show an example to the rest that, in time, will be irresistible?

The idea is attractive: but communal living is not easy; and almost impossible to achieve without some degree of parasitic dependence on existing society.

Philosophical anarchism of this type has a respectable ancestry. William Godwin, writing in Britain 200 years ago, wanted, like the young anarchists of today, to end, or at least severely to limit, organised government: with people living simply and in harmony. He wrote [3]:

> Government, is an evil, an usurpation upon the private judgement and individual conscience of mankind. It were earnestly to be desired that each man was wise enough to govern himself without the intervention of any compulsory restraint, and since government, even in its best state is an evil, the object principally to be aimed at is that we should have as little of it as the general peace of human society will permit.

Property should be equally shared, said Godwin:

> Nothing could be more iniquitous than for one man to possess superfluities while there is in existence a human being not adequately supplied. . . . It is unjust if one man be deprived of leisure to cultivate his rational powers while another contribute not a single effort to add to the common stock.

If luxuries were banned and everyone shared in production, a half-hour's work a day would be sufficient.

> Every man would have a frugal, yet wholesome diet; every man would go forth to that moderate exercise of his corporal functions that would give hilarity to the spirits; none would be made torpid with fatigue but all would have leisure to cultivate the kindly and philanthropic affections of the soul and to let loose his faculties in the search of intellectual improvement.

Godwin sought the decentralisation of society into small local units. His more responsible followers today work in 'syndicates' — small groups of producers or professional workers (e.g. teachers) where a strong solidarity can be generated and good work done: but they reject the political system. One admires the people who set out on this difficult path. Their emphasis on personal responsibility, on the dangers of political democracy, on the debilitating effect of superfluities, on the search for intellectual improvement, perhaps on the need to cultivate 'the philanthropic affections of the soul', is salutary. But one wonders what possibility most of us would have to develop these qualities if there were no political system, no government, to support our efforts.

Some of Godwin's advice is certainly rejected by the more noisy anarchists today. 'We must,' he wrote, 'carefully distinguish between informing people and inflaming them. Indignation, resentment and fury are to be deprecated, and all we should ask is sober thought, clear discernment and intrepid discussion.'

For most of us, the existing political and economic system offers a way forward: provided we are prepared to work for it. With sober thought, clear discernment and intrepid discussion, followed by resolute political action, the advances made in this century can be repeated and surpassed. Of course, mistakes will inevitably be made: but knowledge and inspiration help, and perhaps this book may have provided some.

Questions *for discussion and action*
1. The author picks out some items of Conservative, Socialist and Anarchist ideology for commendation. Does it follow from this that all existing parties could and should fuse? Or is it merely that the parties influence each other's thinking?
Give examples of the influence of one party on the thinking of another.
2. Are there any gross injustices in this country today that should, in your opinion, be resisted. What means of resistance would you employ? Do you agree with the dictum 'the greater the violence, the less the change'? Consider the action of the IRA, Peter Hain and other campaigners.
3. Consider any examples of communal living that are known to you. A number of agricultural communities were set up by conscientious objectors in the Second World War. Some are still running. Find out what you can about them. Do you think it possible to live in a commune in this country today without being a parasite on the rest of society? Does this matter to the members? To the rest of society?
4. William Godwin characterised all government as evil. Find out what particular actions of government led him to this view in 1793. What changes have taken place since then in *(a)* the franchise, *(b)* the party system, and *(c)* the acts now deemed appropriate for governments to undertake. From the results of your investigations and the evidence of this book, do you think that Godwin's view is, or is not, valid today?
5. What, in your opinion, are the strengths and weaknesses of our present form of government described as 'representative, participant, Parliamentary democracy'?

Chapter 20

Suggestions for further reading

20.1 Newspapers and periodicals

Readers of this book will no doubt wish to keep up to date by reading a sensible newspaper. It is a good plan to sample, say, *The Times, The Guardian* and the *Daily Telegraph* for a week each, then to take regularly the one found to be most informative and interesting — and, of course, comprehensible. The 'tasting' might well be done in the college or public library. It is interesting, if one has the time, to look at all three papers for some days and note how they deal with items like student grants, affairs in Parliament, or European news.

The weekly reviews may also be sampled in the libraries: *The Statesman* (social-democrat) *Tribune* (socialist), and further to the Left *The Newsletter* (socialist labour league), *Socialist Worker* (international socialists), *The Militant*, etc. On the Right are the *Spectator* and *The Economist* (rather solid). Non-partisan papers like *The Listener* (with reports of selected BBC broadcasts), and *New Society* (sociology for the layman), appeal to some.

20.2 Books on government and politics

Readers wishing to study further should begin building up their own library, particularly of paper-back books.

On the machinery of government and its operation *The British Constitution made Simple*, by Colin S. Padfield (W. H. Allen, 1970) gives the facts in greater detail than is possible in a book like this. It is clearly and concisely set out. Classic studies of British general elections have been made by David Butler, a familiar figure on television. His *General Election 1970* (with Michael Pinto-Duschinski, Macmillan, 1971) is useful as is *Political Change in Britain* (with Donald Stokes, Macmillan, 1969). The latter looks at the factors operating in society (such as differences in the birth rate as between social classes) and forecasts the long-term effects these may have on support for the political parties.

Voters, Parties and Leaders, by J. Blondel (Penguin, 1966) takes a sociological look at government and politics; that is, it first examines the social structure of the country and examines the electors, the parties and the politicians in the light of it. It is full of interesting information and speculations about social changes and their impact on the political system.

'The Law' is a topic that fascinates some readers. *The Queen's Courts*, by Peter Archer (Penguin, 1965) is a readable account of the history and working of the courts, though some changes have taken place since it was written. *Crime and Society*, by Ben Whitaker (Blond Educational, 1967) considers the social causes of crime, and discusses the treatment of offenders: it is very interestingly written and well illustrated. *Crime in a Changing Society*, by Howard Jones (Penguin, 1967) makes a psychological approach to the problem, assessing the individual offender's responsibility for his actions and making challenging suggestions for changes in his treatment.

The Nature of Politics, by J. D. B. Miller (Penguin, 1967) examines the underlying purpose of politics — the settlement of differences and conflicts — and the ways in which political ideas become effective. Written for the intelligent layman, it is stiff reading but worth it. *British Political Parties*, by Robert Mackenzie (Heinemann, 2nd edition, 1967) examines the structure of the two main political parties and assesses where power lies in each. It notes the similarities in party organisation which have become even more marked since the book was first written. *The Body Politic*, by Ian Gilmour (Hutchinson, 1969) is an interestingly written commentary by a moderate Conservative on the British political system.

The Keynesian revolution, referred to extensively in Part 2 of this book, is dealt with in an understandable way in *Keynes and After*, by Michael Stewart, *not* the former Cabinet Minister! (Penguin, 1967). The present author's *Economics at Work* (Cassell, 1968) gives a straight-forward explanation of many of the topics mentioned here; for example, of Economic Planning, National Income, Prices and Incomes Policy, Balance of Payments, Cost of Living, that arise in so many political discussions.

For those interested in ideas, there is the Fontana Modern

Masters series, extended essays on important thinkers by authoritative writers. One such is by Raymond Williams on *George Orwell*, whose *Animal Farm* and *1984* have been enjoyed by many of today's students. Other 'Masters' in the series are *Bertrand Russell, Gandhi, Guevera*: all worth reading.

20.3 Party statements and official publications

Up-to-date statements of party policy can best be obtained from the parties themselves whose addresses are:
> *Conservative Political Centre*, 32 Smith Square, London W1.
> *Labour Party Publishing Department*, Transport House, Smith Square, London W1.
> *The Liberal Publicity Department*, 7 Exchange Court, London WC2.
> *The Communist Party*, 16 King Street, London WC2.

Organisations outside the parties that publish interesting and often original views are:
> *Conservative:*
> > *The Bow Group*, 240 High Holborn, London WC1.
> *Socialist:*
> > *The Fabian Society*, 11 Dartmouth Street, London SW1.
> *Parliamentary Affairs:*
> > *The Hansard Society*, 162 Buckingham Palace Road, London SW1.

Readers will find of interest the daily or weekly *Hansard*, the verbatim report of Parliamentary debates, available in most public libraries. A visit to the Government Bookshop, 49 High Holborn, London WC1, or its provincial branch offices where the publications of Her Majesty's Stationery Office are on sale, is a fascinating experience. Booklets on an enormous range of topics, interestingly produced and illustrated, are available at reasonable prices.

20.4 Books about people

Politics is about personalities as well as policies. And what personalities some of them were! Therefore there is much interest, not to say amusement — even scandalisation — to be had from reading the lives of statesmen and politicians. The reader might well start with *Britain's Prime Ministers from Walpole to Wilson*, by E. Royston Pike (Odhams, 1968) then read further about the men who have interested him. There is a fascinating study of *Disraeli*, the Tory, by George Blake (Eyre and

Spottiswood, 1968), telling how that extraordinary man, at first thought by many Conservatives to be a charlatan and bounder, became their trusted and revered leader. Much has, of course, been written by or about *Sir Winston Churchill* and his adventures as a young man have been seen in the cinema. Another Conservative, *Mr Harold Macmillan* who was Prime Minister from 1957—63, has written five volumes of autobiography, all well worth reading. As a young man in Parliament between the wars he was distressed by the unemployment in his constituency, Stockton-on-Tees, and advocated unorthodox economic policies which put him at odds with his party. In the Second World War he was the British Cabinet's representative on the spot in North Africa and showed independence and courage (he once burnt a telegram from Churchill) in dealing with the prickly General de Gaulle and in restoring order in Italy, after its defeat. Later volumes deal with the period since the war including his years as Prime Minister.

On the Labour side is *Harold Wilson*'s massive volume *The Labour Government 1964—1970* (Weidenfeld & Nicholson, 1972) a blow-by-blow account of the struggles of himself and his colleagues to tackle the economic and political problems that succeeded one another without pause during their term of office. This is a book to dip into: select some incidents like the tussle with Ian Smith on HMSs *Tiger* and *Fearless* over Rhodesia or the incident with Mr Kosygin of the USSR at Chequers, where Mr Wilson sought to launch a Vietnam peace initiative. Try, also, Mr Wilson's account of George Brown's resignation — and *George Brown's* own account in *In My Way* (Gollancz, 1971). This is the very stuff of politics.

For keen trade unionists there is the study of *Ernest Bevin* by Alan Bullock (Heinemann). Part 1 deals with his rise as a trade-union leader and the foundation of the Transport and General Workers' Union; Part 2 with his term as Minister of Labour in Mr Churchill's coalition war-time Cabinet. He was a tough character, not to be bullied and could stand up to men like Lord Beaverbrook or to Churchill himself.

Young socialists may like to go back to Michael Foot's *Aneurin Bevan 1897—1945* (McGibbon & Kee, 1962) and Vol. II 1945—60 (Davis—Poynter, 1973) and to William Stewart's *Life of Keir Hardie* (ILP, 1921) which inspired earlier socialists.

20.5 History

So much of our condition today springs from action taken in the nineteenth century that some readers may wish to read more about it. There is an interesting series *Society and Industry in the 19th Century*, a documentary approach, edited by Keith Dawson and Peter Wall

(Oxford University Press, 1970) which covers Parliamentary Representation, Factory Reform, Trade Unions, Education, The Problem of Poverty and Public Health and Housing. Here one can see many of the social services that we take for granted today, struggling into life.

An interesting study of social and political reformers who stung apathetic governments into action is Frank Huggett's *Nineteenth Century Reformers* (Oxford University Press, 1970), which gives source material on men like William Cobbett, Sir Edwin Chadwick, Lord Shaftesbury, Keir Hardie and others referred to briefly in this book.

The point about reading is that there is no end to the pleasure to be had from it: one is led on from one book to another, from one author and subject to another. In books one can meet interesting people, share their experiences, their ideas and aspirations; see how they struggled to create a pleasanter, fairer, more civilised Britain: perhaps inspiring ourselves to efforts to the same civilising ends.

References

Chapter 1
1. A. Smith *The Wealth of Nations* (1775).
2. K. Marx. *Manifesto of the Communist Party* (1848). (Quoted in M. Oakshott. *Political Doctrines of Contemporary Europe,* Basis Books, London, 1940, p. 86.)

Chapter 2
1. Economist Intelligence Unit. *The National Newspaper Industry,* 1966, pp. 21, 29, 52.
2. *op. cit.,* p. 31.
3. BBC *Taste and Standards in BBC Programmes,* Feb. 1973.
4. B. Crick. *Political Theory and Practice,* Allen Lane, The Penguin Press, 1971, pp. 51–2.

Chapter 4
1. *The Life and Struggles of William Lovett,* McGibbon and Kee, 1967, p. 307.

Chapter 6
1. Ian Gilmour. *The Body Politic,* Hutchinson, 1969, p. 296.

Chapter 8
1. E. Burke. *Speeches and Letters on American Affairs,* Everyman Library, No. 340, p. 72.
2. E. Summerskill. *A Woman's World,* Heinemann, 1967, p. 54.

Chapter 11
1. Ian Gilmour. *The Body Politic*, Hutchinson, 1969, p. 349.

Chapter 12
1. T. Hobbes. *Leviathan* (1651), Everyman Library, No. 691, pp. 64—5.
2. E. Burke. *Collected Works.* Quoted in *The Tory Tradition*, Butler, p. 39 (see below).
3. B. Disraeli. *Sybil, or The Two Nations*, 1845.
4. Sir G. G. Butler. *The Tory Tradition*, Conservative Political Centre, 1957, p. 63.

Chapter 13
1. J. Locke. *Of Civil Government* (1690), Everyman Library, No. 751, pp. 120, 166.
2. H. N. Brailsford. *Socialism for Today*, Independent Labour Party, 1925, p. 141.
3. R. H. Tawney. *Equality*, Allen and Unwin, 1938, p. 127.
4. C. L. Mowat. *Britain Between the Wars*, Methuen, 1955, p. 261.
5. Women's Group on Public Welfare and National Council of Social Service. *Our Towns*, Oxford University Press, 1944, p. xv.
6. C. L. Mowat. *op. cit.*, p. 205.
7. G. B. Shaw. *The Intelligent Woman's Guide to Socialism and Capitalism*, Constable, 1928.

Chapter 14
1. J. M. Keynes. *The General Theory of Employment, Interest and Money*, Macmillan, 1936.
2. Sir W. Beveridge. *Full Employment in a Free Society*, Allen and Unwin, 1944.
3. D. Dillard. *The Economics of J. M. Keynes*, Crosbie Lockwood, 1948, p. 128.
4. H. Wilson. Speech at Birmingham, 19 January 1964.
5. H. Wilson. Speech at Albert Hall, London, 5 April 1964.

Chapter 15
1. L. J. Callaghan, Chancellor of the Exchequer, 5 October 1966.
2. *The British Economy, Key Statistics 1900—1970.* Published for the London and Cambridge Economic Service by Times Newspapers Ltd. Table B (G.D.P. at Fixed Prices).
3. R. H. Jenkins, Chancellor of the Exchequer, Budget Speech, 19 March 1968.

References

4. R. H. Jenkins, Chancellor of the Exchequer, Budget Speech, 15 April 1969.
5. R. H. Jenkins, Chancellor of the Exchequer, Budget Speech, 15 April 1969.
6. *Monthly Digest of Statistics*, No. 3, 27, March 1973, HMSO, Table 143.

Chapter 16

1. Lord Coleraine. *For Conservatives Only*, Tom Stacey, 1970, pp. 153—4.
2. E. Powell. Speech at Bromsgrove, 6 July 1963. (Quoted with others, below from *A Nation Not Afraid; The Thinking of Enoch Powell*, E. J. Ward (ed.), Batsford, 1965.)
3. E. Powell. *The Observer*, December 1963.
4. E. Powell. Speech at Dulwich, 29 February 1964.
5. E. Powell. Speech at Wolverhampton, 25 September 1964.
6. E. Powell. Speech at Bosworth, 31 August 1968.
7. E. Powell. Speech at Bromsgrove, 6 July 1963.
8. Lord Coleraine. *op. cit.*, pp. 156, 130—1, 131, 144.
9. P. Worsthorne. *Conservatism Today*, Conservative Political Centre, 1966, p. 29.
10. *The Labour Government's Economic Record*, W. Beckerman (ed.), Duckworth, 1972.
11. *Labour and Inequality.* Fabian Essays, Peter Townsend and Nicholas Bosanquet (eds.), Fabian Society, 1972.
12. *May Day Manifesto, 1968.* Raymond Williams (ed.), Pelican, 1968.

Chapter 18

1. D. Butler and D. Stokes. *Political Change in Britain*, Macmillan, 1969, Table 4.7, p. 77.
2. M. Abrams. *Class Distinction in Britain*, Conservative Political Centre, 1958. (Quoted in Blondel, below, as Table 13.)
3. Eric A. Nordlinger. *Working Class Tories*, McGibbon and Kee, 1967.
4. J. Blondel. *Voters, Parties and Leaders*, Pelican, 1966.
5. *National Opinion Polls.* (Quoted in Butler and King, *The British General Election, 1966*, Macmillan, 1967.)
6. R. Rose. *The Times*, 20 June 1970.
7. J. Blondel. *op. cit.* (Table 14, p. 59.)
8. Goldthorpe, Lockwood *et al. The Affluent Worker*, CUP, 1968.
9. R. Rose. *Influencing Voters: A Study of Campaigning Rationality*, Faber, 1967, p. 114.

10.   *op. cit.*, p. 57.

Chapter 19
   1.   John Donne. *Devotions XVII*.
   2.   H. J. Laski. *Liberty in the Modern State*, Pelican, 1937, pp. 91−2.
   3.   Wm. Godwin. *An Enquiry Concerning the Principles of Political Justice and its Influence on General Virtue and Happiness, 1793*. (Quoted in George Woodcock's *Biography of Wm. Godwin*, Porcupine Press.)

Index